I0167028

# BRITAIN UNDER SHELLFIRE

### By
## FRANK ILLINGWORTH

*Contributor to:*
*Chambers Journal, London Evening News, Men Only, National Review, Star, Sphere, Sunday Dispatch and Provincial papers; also the Toronto Star, New Zealand Mirror, Sydney Morning Herald and other Empire Publications.*

*The writer, with his home in Dover, has witnessed every long-range shelling of the Dover area from the first bombardment to quite recently. Facts herein, which are up to date, have been passed by the censor.*

## The Naval & Military Press Ltd

*Published by*

## The Naval & Military Press Ltd

Unit 5 Riverside, Brambleside
Bellbrook Industrial Estate
Uckfield, East Sussex
TN22 1QQ England

Tel: +44 (0)1825 749494

www.naval-military-press.com
www.nmarchive.com

*In reprinting in facsimile from the original, any imperfections are inevitably reproduced
and the quality may fall short of modern type and cartographic standards.*

# CONTENTS

# INTRODUCTION

THIS pen is taken up not in the writer's capacity as a free-lance journalist reporting on the war, but as a resident of a bomb-, bullet- and shell-tormented town recording glimpses of daily affairs from the moment the first German shells soared across the Straits of Dover to drop from a height of 40,000 feet on to British homes. He embarks upon the subject with temerity, for the reactions to bombardment of the Dover-area's men, women, children and even animals are recorded by many famous American and British War Correspondents. But they observe from the purely analytical aspect of professional journalists and in this he finds an excuse for poising his pen. For Dover is his home town; and many of the folk who flit through these pages are his friends.

The Battle of the Big Guns has until recently been shrouded in mystery. *Communiqués* on the subject of shelling by batteries of the great weapons said to be spaced 90 to 100 yards apart along the French coast from Calais to Dunkirk have been no more communicative than those concerning the activities of our south-eastern "Bosche Busters." Much of that recorded herein would not have passed the Censor three months ago. Reporting on air raids differs fundamentally from recording the boundless spleen of enemy long-range artillerymen. A few ill-chosen words could easily lose Britain a round in the Battle of the Channel Guns, and for this reason the Censor has rightly clipped the wings of the journalistically inquisitive. And only now, nearly eighteen months after the first 14-inch high explosive cabers exploded among British homes, has part of an exciting chapter in British history been released for publication.

The writer presents it in *Britain Under Shellfire,* and if upon occasion the first person pronoun creeps into the narrative, will his readers excuse him on the grounds that he witnessed the writing of a paragraph in British history: the Bombardment of Britain.

# CHAPTER ONE

## THE FIRST BOMBARDMENTS

THE explosion of the first German shells in the Dover area ran up the spine of the nation like an electric shock as by telegraph, telephone, rail and road the news sped to the foremost corners of the island. Never before in her long, strenuous and hectically colourful history had Britain suffered bombardment by *land* batteries. Vikings and Jutes and Danes and Saxons, Romans and Normans, Frenchmen, Dutchmen, Spaniards—and even Italians— had thrust at our seagirt shores to pillage and burn and kill and retreat before the unrivalled fury of the Briton attacked on his own soil. Coming nearer modern times the first World War saw German men-o'-war steam past Hartlepool and Scarborough, guns blazing; witnessed a German destroyer flotilla pump 200 shells into what it fondly thought was Dover (Channel "drift" or jittery German nerves sending the shells into the cliffs). But never before had Britain been shelled by *land* batteries: never had she even been under their callous stare. Her people's scanty knowledge of artillery bombardment, of shell-scarred homes, shell-pocked roads and shell-shattered nerves was presented by an adventurous band of special writers and news cameramen: insulated from the Continent by a narrow strip of tumbled water they surveyed the world and its troubles from the security of reading-rooms and cinema seats until one historically memorable day the colourful pageantry of Britain's history was enlarged by the "crump" of shells exploding among the peoples' homes. And the first explosions jerked their brains into a full appreciation of the facts: *German guns were but 6½ leagues distant.*

Suddenly they realised the utter futility of the old conception that because the English flag fluttered from Dover Castle for nine centuries neither the Archangel Gabriel nor Lucifer nor the latter's human counterpart would have the caddish impudence to try and shoot it down according to his conceptions of "cricket"! Suddenly it was realised that while England pondered whether or not to recognise the new rules a powerful enemy knocked on the Gateway to Britain with modern battering-rams: high explosive shells.

5

Few events following the fall of France brought home with such "shattering" reality the nearness of the enemy to our portals as the first shelling of Britain. The smashing of the B.E.F. was something presented in the papers: even the fall of Calais with its accompaniment of gunfire heard across the Channel presented an unreal picture. The fires seen were a long way off. Here, however, was something very concrete. Britain lay beneath the shadow of German land batteries: they had London within reach.

Just as the march of science rendered this island a target for the bomber, so it brought the fair face of Kent and the Metropolis within range of land artillery. And overnight Dover labelled with a new meaning the music hall joke that "Dover is a nice little town near Germany"!

Dover was fortified by the Romans and Normans. The former named it Portus Duris; the latter called it Dovere, both of which names were variations of the Celtic word "Dour," the name of a muddy little stream running through the town. For nine centuries its fine castle, resting on foundations 2,000 years old, brooded over the town from the heights . . . solid testimony that this is the Gateway to England through which no enemy has passed since the Bastard King, though time and again its defenders, anticipating attack, peered across the Channel.

History repeats itself. Thursday, August 22, 1940, saw watching eyes survey British merchantmen steaming through the straits in an easterly direction. A perfect day, cooled by a mellow breeze, the sun shining from a blue sky framed in cumulus cloud. Against this tranquil background gulls sailed, insects hummed busily, errand boys meandered in the manner common to their ilk. The world was at war, but to-day even sirens were silent.

But not only from the Castle did eyes watch the convoy. Twenty-one miles away the Teuton peered through prismatic binoculars at eighteen ships steaming in close formation towards the "Gate" in the Channel minefield off Folkestone. By simple mathematical calculations their range was ascertained: the order given to fire.

The convoy was continuously shelled from a point off Dungeness to another slightly east of Dover.

At exactly 11 a.m., August 22, 1940, the silence was shattered by heavy explosions.

"What was that?" Every eye peered skywards. Aerial raiders? No!

The writer sped townwards astride a bicycle "borrowed" from an errand boy. To the tune of three more "booms" his mind subconsciously registered a picture of the lad standing, his mouth agape in amazement at the sudden loss of a bike, a basketful of freshly-baked bread resting against a grubby collar! It's strange how trivialities stand out in moments of anxiety or excitement.

"Hey, Mister! Moi boike!" But he was too late. It carried a part-time fireman towards his station at breakneck speed!

Further heavy explosions greeted his arrival at the first road-block. "Halt! Identity card?" (Dover was noticeably fifth-column conscious in those days). "What's happening, soldier?" "Dunno, buddy, but it don't look good."

Spinning wheels brought the harbour into view, and a convoy. Impressive sight: solid-looking merchantmen of as varied size, shape and colour as their destroyer escorts were uniform. Every few minutes great columns of water leapt up round them to the tune of loud explosions. A warden shouted "Shelling!" as the bicycle carried its borrower from fire station to sea front, where policemen advanced stern warnings to take cover.

By a nearby public lavatory lurked the war correspondent of a famous London daily, and the moment official eyes were turned he and the writer sped across the road and into an empty house and on to its balcony for a grandstand view of the action. By a whelk stall two other correspondents recorded events.

A magnificent sight! Eighteen merchantmen steaming in close order nosed slowly forward, not changing course, not seeming to care about the great fountains of water rising first to port, then to starboard, to fore and aft. Their destroyer escorts sped frantically back and forth, black smoke from funnels and white clouds from smoke buoys mingling to defeat enemy gunners.

Boulogne guns were the first to open up; and as ships entered the Straits so Calais guns fired. Regularly every two minutes pin-points of flame stabbed the faint Channel haze at positions between the two occupied ports.

"Gris Nez guns! It's taking the shells about 65 seconds to cross the Channel. Another salvo's about due." Sure

enough great gouts of water erupted and the roar of
exploding shells crashed against chalk cliffs, rumbled inland,
bringing the mighty voice of Mars to verdant valleys.

One salvo fell dangerously near a destroyer; other high
explosive cabers fell among the convoy; two shells landed
in the harbour, one hard by a minesweeper of the Dover
Patrol; another near the shore, sending at least two watchers
diving for what cover balcony railings offered!

Shells followed the convoy through the Straits. For an
hour German guns roared: 144 shells were fired. But no
direct hit resulted, and as the rumble of artillery fire died
away the Press-haunted Grand Hotel filled up and newspapermen converged on telephones linking them with
highly interested London editors, later to discuss a remark-
able episode in British history over copious tankards of
"Kent's Best".

One point was settled: the enemy could not close the
Straits of Dover to British convoys—at least, not until he
had considerably increased the number of guns across the
Channel. However, the action provided wider aspects.
Dover was agreed that Hun artillery could reduce to a
minimum the value of Dover Harbour; and it had the
town's 13½ square miles of houses, ancient monuments,
streets, parks and playgrounds within its span.

Though many suspected the fact, few local folk outside
the confidence of Authority *knew* Britain had been shelled
previously. On the morning of August 12, 1940, two heavy
explosions followed on the heels of the "All Clear" and two
columns of brick dust soared sullenly over the town. Splinters
and blast claimed the lives of a man, a woman and a dog.

A few days previously shells had landed in the
Folkestone area.

On August 20 it was announced that three craters had been
found on the south-east coast following three loud reports.
People took these to be the bark of A.A. guns or boom
of time-bombs. But not everyone accepted these explana-
tions. The explosions lacked the "crack" of A.A. guns
and the deep roar of bombs. The sky, brilliantly clear,
offered no cover to aerial raiders; and though in these parts
bombing frequently heralds the sirens, meticulous care on
the part of the authorities reduces to a minimum the
possibility of bombs being dropped before sirens scream.
Furthermore, there were no unexploded bombs at the time.

The only alternative was—shells. In view of the tremendous strides made in artillery science since Germans shelled Paris from a range of 74 miles, it was obvious southeast Kent lay within the reach of enemy artillery on the occupied coast: the shelling of the convoy proved that, too. And east Kent had long believed the day would dawn when those guns would be fired at Britain.

Rumours chased each other along the streets, invaded every home, shop, office, public-house and A.R.P. post to emerge decked in more striking garb.

Dover divided itself into three main groups. To old soldiers the explosions conjured up memories of Flanders, and some even swore they heard the whine of missiles soaring overhead: another section of the community favoured the bombing theory—indeed, bombs were *seen* falling. When a London daily printed a paragraph to the effect that "Shells are believed to have been dropped on a south-east coast town by an enemy raider," the gap between those favouring the bombing theory and the old soldiers was bridged.

But this paragraph released another crop of rumours: *the enemy had run out of bombs!*

The third group was disinclined to accept any theory without evidence. This soon arrived: sections of shell casing were found near the scene of the explosions.

So it was shelling! The knowledge started in its wake a third avalanche of rumours—written and spoken.

American papers suggested a 12-inch gun fired at Dover, probably a gun of French origin. (Later, a nose-cap with French markings came into my possession.) The German-controlled Dutch radio told how a four-inch gun fired 30- to 35-lb. shells across the Straits, but London believed the enemy had used larger guns, probably of 12-inch calibre. Between these two extremes, theories as to the size and range of enemy guns were advanced, among them the suggestion that German artillerymen were firing "rocket" shells: the latter theory resulted from the so-called "double report" of the missiles.

Official reticence prevented Dover presenting a uniform opinion until the night of August 22, 1940, ten hours after the convoy was shelled.

Strangely enough, many of us did not at first realise we were being shelled that lovely night. It might be

argued that the detonations of 11 a.m. with those of 9 p.m.
should have been linked.  But there is a wide difference
between the sound of shells bursting in the sea a mile or
so distant, and those exploding on land.  The former
rumble; the latter explode with deafening, ear-splitting
roars ending in thunder-like claps.

So it was that though many folk anticipated being
shelled after the German exhibition that morning, when
enemy guns opened up ten hours later, some were caught
guessing.

The evening of August 22, 1940, was the first occasion
upon which Britain suffered heavy bombardment by long-
range land batteries.  The few shells tossed across the Straits
previously were in the nature of sighting shots, a very lean
dress rehearsal to Thursday, August 22.

\*       \*       \*       \*       \*

I have no need to turn up my diary to recall the occasion: every episode stands out crystal clear.

Nine p.m. saw me listening to the B.B.C.'s account of our
latest "defeat".  The morning's slight breeze had vanished.
Moon and stars fought a winning battle against fading
sunlight.  From nearby trees the tuneful vesper of blackbirds soothed the senses and the hoot of owls lent tone to
advancing night.  Not even a Sistine choir could supplement the song of eventime.  Peace reigned supreme.  At
this tranquility Nazi artillerymen ranged their guns.

The blackbirds' tuneful vesper became shrills of alarm
to their neighbours that all was not well when a mighty
detonation tore the silence asunder.  Three further explosions followed.  My housekeeper and her husband, one,
Stubbs, and I collided in a scramble for the front door.

"The 'sireens' (local pronunciation) haven't gone,
have they?"

"No."  Silence settled on the heels of the last explosion
and we were returning indoors, considerably mystified,
when the house rocked to further detonations close by.

"Crikey-did-you-hear-that?" said Mrs. Stubbs.

Warden Brown (of the Westminster Bank, later to suffer
hits), came running up.  He looked worried.

"Wouldn't be sure, but I think that's shelling.  Listen!
See if we can hear the stuff coming over."  He lay on his
stomach, seeking the shelter of a low wall.  Further roars,
brilliant flashes, and the unexpected descent of several tiles

witnessed Mr. and Mrs. Stubbs' hasty descent into the shelter and my sudden departure for the fire station.

At the bottom of the road Warden Brown was warning the occupants of a car not to venture into the town. He couldn't know it, but actually this was the worst advice possible, for three shells exploded within 800 yards of him for every one in the town.

Every few minutes four-gun salvos burst on Britain. The height of the bombardment saw British bombers raining explosives on enemy gun positions at Cap Gris Nez, St. Inglevert and Audembert. This attack continued on and off from approximately 9.30 p.m. to 3 a.m. British coastal batteries, too, opened up at enemy positions. They seemed to be firing every ten minutes, but owing to the almost continuous A.A. barrage it was difficult to arrive at an accurate conclusion. However, *The Times* stated (next day): "British land guns on Thursday night fired some rounds at the French coast . . . it was authoritatively stated in London last night." This, then, was the first occasion in the history of Britain to see British coastal batteries engage enemy emplacements.

Summer-lightning-like flashes from the direction of Cap Gris Nez warned one to expect explosions on our side of the Channel. Subsequent actions saw A.R.P. personnel proceed to "posts" without stopping unless their routes lay through districts under fire. In the latter instance they kept eyes skinned for tell-tale flashes from France, calculating their positions relative to shelter when the salvos landed in about a minute's time. There was something rather undignified in a few moments' violent pedalling on a bicycle, the sudden forsaking of the saddle for the shelter afforded by a public lavatory or shop doorway, only to remount for a few more moments' pedalling until the next flash was about a minute old! But it added zest to life! And it proved we had learned our lesson that "a dead fireman ain't no good".

This night, however, civilians had no previous experience upon which to lean. They were new to shelling. They were not unlike the wardens who used to shelter from shrapnel when A.A. guns opened up; the same men wander in the open to-day beneath much more severe "steel rain." And so Dover knew not whether to stop and shelter or proceed apace to homes or A.R.P. posts.

Four minutes later a shrapnel shell burst overhead with a clap of thunder and showers of light, and approximately half an hour after the bombardment commenced, sirens wailed a warning. By that time the action had slowed down.

Britain was being shelled. She had entered on a new phase in her history; and her people did not take kindly to the experience.

Previously, the writer's arrival at the fire station had usually been met with remarks unsuited to his position as (even a junior) officer; "Whatcheer, cock," "Here comes Frankie!" and similar banter. But this night there were no smiles, no greetings. The men stood in anxious little groups: voices were low, conversation restricted. Then someone said; *"We're being shelled, Sir!"* The same atmosphere pervaded the control room; Section-Officers Bainton and Campbell, G.M., pretended to play darts: telephonists' knitting-needles clicked rather faster than usual; Patrol-Officer Spicer (a milk roundsman in peace time) pretended to read. Everyone awaited the first "call"; and "Pol", the A.F.S. pet with a marvellous repertoire of warlike sounds, looked more surprised with each explosion. Poor Pol was soon to have his cage flattened by shell-splinter!

Gun flashes showed the streets to be empty: folk had "gone to ground," but before the last German shell exploded they were filtering into the open, standing in silent groups by the wreckage of homes and churches.

The damage was not nearly as extensive as we had imagined it would be. Let me quote from my diary: "Several houses are shattered. One cottage has its wall torn away and everything from beds to mirrors are exposed to view, all jumbled up. Before the bombardment ceased an elderly woman climbed over the rubble to retrieve her night attire. Pathetic! Wicked! A Mrs. Clark was dragged to safety by Fireman F. (more about this violin-playing A.F.S. despatch-rider later). Another shell that laid two sailors low shattered the Catholic church's roof, injured its Canon. But the worst damage was suffered by St. Barnabas' Church. Shattered! While a warden borrowed a fireman's axe to despatch a little dog running round on three legs, howling, knots of folk gaped at the broken walls. Inside—a shambles. A cheap plaster cast of Christ stands on its head near the altar: another plaster cast sways from a chipped beam, holding up chipped arms as if in horror at this sacrilege. Biked into a shell hole on the way home. Must rise early to-morrow to survey damage before the place is cleaned up."

But by 9 a.m. Dover was more or less spick and span . . . if shell-scarred. Rubble and glass were piled in neat heaps. Errand boys whistled on their bicycles: children stopped playing bombing *and* shelling to gather small splinters. People picked up shopping-bags, shouldered spades, sat at typewriters, drank coffee. Mrs. Stubbs exchanged shelling experiences for a pint of milk: the bread and the daily papers arrived on time. At a cost of about £100,000 (calculated at an overall expenditure of £700 per shell fired) Nazi gunners had "knocked Dover's front teeth out": but the town continued to smile.

A few of those who could conveniently leave were planning to evacuate. (My wife and family had long since gone). But there was no question of mass evacuation. Determination to "see it through" overshadowed the prospect of probable further bombardment. Only in one respect had Dover altered: more tin hats were in evidence!

To-day, steel helmets dangle from errand boys' handle-bars, lurk beneath the knees of 'bus drivers, caress the hips of road-sweepers. They symbolise the "carry on" spirit.

Grim as was the episode of August 22, 1940, subsequent events proved it to have been a picnic by comparison. The shell which at 10 a.m. a few days later demolished a house, spared a six-months' old baby only to kill the mother, was followed by intermittent bombardment for forty-eight hours. Fortunately, many of the shells exploded off-shore or in fields. The writer returned home to a belated meal to find Stubbs hobbling to his coal mine. He had been standing at the entrance to the Anderson shelter when the blast from a shell bursting 300 yards away (killing a horse) shot him into the shelter on his hip, and opened up his leg below the knee.

That night the R.A.F. went into action, apparently against enemy gun positions. The air reverberated with the thunder of war from occupied France. At such times pressmen line the cliffs, recording episodes fit to warm the hearts of sorely-tried Londoners.

But German long-range guns, hidden in tunnels and woods, and adequately protected by A.A. batteries, are hard to silence. We have reason to believe some have been spiked by R.A.F. bombs and British shells, but others still poke their snouts in the direction of Dover.

As much perhaps to fit them for the coming blitz on London (remember, the capital had not as yet suffered heavy raids) as to relieve tired men, a batch of firemen drawn from several London fire stations arrived in Dover in exchange for a Dover squad.

The Londoners behaved like children at cockshies! They gazed, awe-struck, at the A.A. barrage which in those days earned the south-east of England the name "Hell's Corner": crashing planes sent them into ecstasies of delight: flaming barrage balloons fascinated them. Soon some of these fellows were killed in London.

By a strange twist of fate, Dover's tired crews arrived in London to suffer the first blitz and the Londoners had a taste of heavy bombardment from occupied France.

The day in question proved ominously quiet until the evening. There was an unusual lack of alerts. Six p.m. saw the Press-haunted Grand Hotel—later to be damaged by several direct hits—crammed to capacity, men "swilling beer," as Jo-Jo, the blonde London barmaid, expressed it. At 6.11 showers of shingle from a shell on the beach cascaded down to the roar of high explosives.

This was to be a severe bombardment, or what was considered severe in those days. Of the 140-odd shells reported to have arrived from a height of 40,000 feet and a distance of twenty-one miles (or more), sixty-five exploded between 6.11 p.m. and 7.45. The first stage ended at 6.37: British bombers appeared to be in action. But at 7.8 enemy guns spoke again.

The A.F.S. arranged for a volunteer to man an observation post at Dover Castle as soon as shelling began. From there H.Q. was informed by 'phone of the approximate position of shell bursts. This post offered considerable scope. If shells fell in the town one saw columns of brick dust soaring skywards; pinpoints of flame from occupied France heralded the arrival of each salvo. One knew when they were coming: one could only await their arrival; fume at the futility of it all, curse at one's impotence to *do* anything other than lift the receiver.

·· Enemy gunners did not appear to have any definite

target in mind: they were ranging over the whole "area."
Approximately every two minutes four-gun salvos crashed
among our homes. One anticipated their arrival to within
seconds. My diary reads: "Four shells at 6.11 p.m.;
6.13 four shells; 6.15 four shells; 6.19 four shells" and so on
to 6.37.

Darkness saw hell let loose. The sky flickered with
"summer lightning" as our guns replied to German fire:
from the heights splashes of light from German guns were
followed by the flash of exploding shells in Kent, while
a continuous stream of A.A. fire from the "other side"
was every now and again doused for split seconds by the
flash of British bombs: between the roar of our heavy
coastal batteries and the crack of German shells there came
the deep rumble of bombing from occupied France. It was
impossible to differentiate with any accuracy between
the various sounds in this mixed brew of noise. It continued
for roughly an hour and a half. But not until well past
midnight did complete silence return.

Meanwhile the streets were clear except for A.R.P.
personnel, police and a few Servicemen. On account of the
many people caught away from home by the shelling, pubs
did a roaring trade. Shelters were full. The men's quarters
at the fire station were crammed with women and children
to such an extent that "off-duty" men—those awaiting
a call—were unable to play billiards!

Only one little girl reflected her mother's nervousness,
and I have a mental picture of a husky London fireman
rescuing her from tears with a hastily concocted fairy
story! By eleven o'clock most of the kiddies were sharing
blankets with off-duty men, or monopolising their steel
beds with their mothers.

And the results of this bombardment? Considerable
damage to private property. One London fireman bowled
over with a brick in the back; and four people killed.

That night taught Dover that while German shells
must be respected, the bark of enemy guns is worse than
their bite. We soon learned that weight for weight the
effect of shells is less than that of bombs. Shell damage is
accentuatedly "local." "Splinter shells" spray considerable
areas with deadly "rain," but buildings which would nor-
mally collapse under the impact of 1,000 lb. bombs, stand
up remarkably well to shells weighing approximately

1,500 lbs. However, though blast from the latter is noticeably less than that of heavy bombs, damage caused by flying
splinters is more accentuated in the case of shells.

Shelling has other disadvantages as compared with
bombing. Even in this outpost, where bombers can so easily
unload without "springing the siren," "Wailing Willie"
usually gives a few moments' warning. Enemy daylight
raiders can be *seen*, bombs watched on their descent and
lightning calculations made accordingly. Even at night the
possibility of bombing is heralded by the drone of enemy
raiders and the bark of A.A. guns. Furthermore, once
bombs have been dropped enemy raiders no longer hold
one's full respect.

Shelling, on the other hand, presents an entirely different
aspect. Except at night (and only then if one is so placed
to see flashes from occupied territory) there is no warning.
Contrary to the general belief, shells give no audible warning
of their approach. Only when missiles pass directly overhead to burst inland do they fulfil the popular conception,
and even then explosions precede the whine of the shells—
an eerie, high-pitched warble.

In their cross-Channel flight shells attain the sub-
stratosphere, falling on to their targets from a height
of approximately 40,000 feet at a speed in excess of sound.
Consequently, one is frequently caught in the open when
enemy guns fire; indeed, towards the end of 1940 it was not
uncommon for meals, sleep, bath, work and pleasure to be
suddenly terminated by enemy shelling.

October 27, 1940, saw the shell-fire warning introduced—
an alert followed by a second alert—and the erection of
black-and-yellow notice boards at all arterial entrances to
areas under fire: SHELLING IN PROGRESS: TAKE COVER,
a stern warning frequently ignored by pedestrian and
motorist alike. But by this time the shell-fire warning
proved redundant. Dover labelled the explosion of shells
with unfailing accuracy: even animals learned to distinguish
between bomb and shell. The latter's boom is unmistakable.

Just as opening phases of bombardments cannot be
anticipated, so their duration is a matter of speculation.
A.R.P. personnel run sweepstakes on the probable duration
of an action, but winners are not paid until well after
sirens sound the all-clear. The reason for this seeming
reticence on the part of "bankers" to meet their obligations

is explained by the fact that all-clears too frequently hear the arrival of further salvos. The all-clear is sounded a stipulated time after the arrival of what appears to be the last shell of a bombardment, but it does not always mark the termination of enemy action. Not infrequently Fleet Street reports that "After an hour's lull the Dover area was shelled for a further half-hour to-day," or words to that effect. Often a lull is read as the end of the day's "fun and games"; shelters disgorge their occupants and tin hats are doffed as further salvos arrive!

One such occasion heard the all-clear sounded approximately an hour after the arrival of the last shell. Cadaverous Leading-hand Philpott proceeded from the fire station to his home for a long-overdue meal. The streets were full again (indeed, the bombardment had not been sufficiently heavy to clear them entirely, even at its height) and sirens had barely died when a roar was followed by showers of brick fragments. Several girls dodged under cover, a woman with a pram scuttled into a shop doorway, Philpott dropped from his bicycle to remount hurriedly and pedal back to the fire station. No more shells followed that day: the second all-clear proved to have read the enemy's mind correctly.

But at any moment his guns might have opened up again. Life is like that in Dover.

## CHAPTER TWO

### THE BATTLE OF THE BIG GUNS

CROSS-CHANNEL shelling has proved a topic of debate since German long-range weapons first fired across the Straits of Dover in August, 1940. Each shelling revives the same queries. How many batteries capable of spanning the Straits has the enemy at his disposal? What are their purpose? Does our side of the Channel boast as heavy armament? What is the military and naval significance of cross-Channel guns?

Obviously these questions cannot be answered fully at the present time: some local knowledge would not pass the Censor, and particulars local people would like to have are not released for publication. Reporting on air raids differs fundamentally from recording the activities of enemy

★

long-range artillerymen.    A few ill-chosen words could easily guide shells to their objectives.

The Front known as the Dover area extends inland and to either side of the town, including that area of the southeast within the known range of enemy land batteries, in consequence of which Dover residents are often unable to enlarge on Press reports to the effect that "the Dover area was shelled again to-day." Indeed, shells have burst within the perimeter fortifications without Doverians learning the reason for, or the results of, the bombardment! Especially does this apply at night, when cinema seats, public-house stools or beds shudder to the roar of exploding shells.

Local authorities are reticent on the question of cross-Channel shelling: *communiqués* on the subject, even when residents have concrete evidence of the results of bombardment, are invariably restricted to a few words, and a majority of Press reports are laced with such phrases as "It is believed that . . ." or "It is thought locally . . ."

Such paragraphs are based on conjecture. But of one thing we can be sure: *The primary purpose of German cross-Channel guns was to close the Straits of Dover to British shipping.*

Pre-war days saw roughly 40 per cent of Britain's imports reach her via the Dover Straits. Bearing this in mind it can be understood why the threatened fall of French Channel Ports in 1916 was a serious matter. Approximately 200,000 vessels negotiated the Straits during the Great War, carrying vital supplies to East Coast ports.

The Channel *had* to be kept open. It was stated that with the enemy controlling the 21-miles' wide Straits, 20,000,000 additional tons of merchandise would converge on west coast ports annually; insufficient dock facilities and warehouse space would seriously retard its unloading, while the carrying of such vast additional tonnage to London, the south-east and part of the east coast, might have proved sufficiently complex to necessitate the evacuation of one third of the population westwards.

The question of evacuation does not arise to-day. Long before French Channel ports fell in 1940's Spring, large sections of the community had already been moved westwards. Nevertheless, the closing of the Dover Straits to British convoys could have more than nuisance value, to-day; the very time lost in sailing round the north of Scotland (by-passing western ports to prevent congestion) to east coast docks would place additional strain on our war effort. And so, once in possession of French Channel ports, the enemy sought to supplement his U-boats, mine-fields, E-boats and dive-bombers with long-range guns in an endeavour to seal the Straits of Dover.

A vain endeavour! Despite the three to four thousand shells fired at British Channel convoys by Calais guns and the many thousand bombs aimed at them, the Merchant Navy still ploughs through the narrow bottle-neck separating France and Britain.

French coastal batteries formed the nucleus of German long-range artillery opposite Dover. But the number of guns has been increased with German-made weapons; and if we are to accept Press reports, by heavy artillery from the Maginot line. We know enemy guns are mounted near Calais, by Cap Gris Nez lighthouse and the Dover Patrol Memorial at Gravelines, St. Inglevert, Audembert, Floringazelles and farther down Channel towards Boulogne. On clear days I have watched coils of yellow smoke rising from their muzzles, and since they first fired across the Straits their positions have been pin-pointed by flash-spotting and sound location.

Boulogne guns were the first to engage a British convoy . . . on August 22, 1940. Eighteen merchantmen drew their fire at a point off Dungeness lighthouse, and as the ships nosed slowly through the Straits behind a smoke screen, so enemy guns facing them opened up until Calais batteries terminated the bombardment with four-gun salvos. One hundred and forty shells were fired, at a cost of about £100,000, without a single direct hit being scored.

The enemy followed up his initial effort to close the Dover Straits with artillery fire by a violent dive-bombing attack on the convoy off Deal. In the subsequent hurly-burly Deal saw the 1,000th plane in the Battle for Britain brought down.

The enemy knows his dive-bombers have attained more in a few hectic seconds than his long-range guns have accomplished in hours of shelling.

To watch bombs rained on Channel shipping stirs one to fury. Those seamen, sometimes little over three miles off-shore, suffer hell on earth while from the safety of

cliff-tops and once tourist-thronged sea-fronts one watches
plane after plane "peel off" with its deadly cargo. Bombs
drop: ships vanish behind great gouts of water to emerge
bobbing like corks in a furious sea: ships suffer direct hits
to founder before one's eyes and there is nothing to do but
watch them sink.

One day I stood among a group of Norwegian seamen
rescued from a mined merchantman. Nearby a girl stood
with her hand to her throat. The Norwegian wearing a
nasty scar turned to her and in halting English said: "It—
is—not—good—to—see——" He spoke for all of us. On
another occasion Folkestone fishermen murmured "Swines!
"Swines!" as they put off in small boats to lend a hand.
This feeling of impotent fury at dive-bombing attacks on
convoys is universal in the south-east.

Officers and men of the Channel convoys stand high
among the heroes of the Second World War. Their job is
utterly different from that suffered by deep-sea sailors.
Atlantic convoys run the gauntlet of U-boats, surface
raiders and bombers; but their crews enjoy periods of
bright lights and safety in foreign ports. Not so Channel
sailors. They have no rest. As soon as a cargo is delivered
they put-about, sail—or should I say steam?—through the
Straits again, right under the noses of enemy gunners and
within four minutes' flying of German aerodromes.

Not for some time after the first shelling of a Channel
convoy in August, 1940, did the enemy support his dive-
bombers with coastal batteries in efforts to close the
Straits. Probably he was prompted in this by the considerable losses in planes and pilots inflicted by A.A. guns
and fighter patrols. Towards the end of 1940 our aerial
predominance over the Channel became noticeable: we
saw more and more British fighter patrols. By the Spring
of '41 it was firmly established, and dive-bombers intent
on destroying Channel convoys ran the gauntlet of multiple
cannon guns. Thirteen machines have been shot down in
one attack on Dover Harbour. And *that* was a sight to
cheer! Even more noticeable was British air superiority
by August, 1941. Whereas a year before the Dover area
suffered constant battles overhead (it knew twelve sirens
in one day), twelve months later it was we who carried the
air initiative. In fact, when my wife returned to Dover
for a holiday in August '41, the policemen who examined

her papers at Priory Station said: "The last siren? Oh, I'd say about a week ago. We go 'over there' now."

1941's Spring and Summer saw the enemy resorting to his coastal batteries more frequently. And though his *communiqués* not infrequently claimed to have scattered or sunk merchantmen, we saw no evidence to substantiate all his claims. In a rumour-conscious town even rumours about shell-damaged merchantmen were noticeably scarce.

The crews of Channel convoys show a decided distaste for shelling. It is not unusual to hear weather-beaten (and sometimes white-haired) masters cursing German gunners in the roundest seafaring terms. One night an irate seaman brought blushes to the cheeks of a B.B.C. star in the dingy little Hippodrome Bar, causing "Auntie," the then barmaid, to squash him severely. Auntie could be relied upon to keep order among the motley crowds of sailors, soldiers, airmen, nurses, Service girls, strip-tease artistes, chorus girls, B.B.C. impersonators, musicians and comedians sharing its fœtid atmosphere. The Hip' "artists' bar" was little patronised in pre-war days, but war transformed it into the focal point of Dover's night life.

But if merchantmen curse German gunners, at least they only suffer bombardment while negotiating the Straits, and not always then. Not so the Dover Patrol.

The enemy is gaining no useful information by reading that Dover Harbour is now only used by light naval craft: *Luftwaffe* pilots and balloon observers soaring over Calais keep him well informed on its marine contents. And the "little ships" live under the shadow of German artillery.

Sometimes they're shelled in the harbour: sometimes at sea while patiently, yard by yard and with infinite toil and patience, they sweep passages for our convoys.

One day I watched high explosive shells bursting round three mine-sweepers not a mile off-shore: they were almost lifted out of the water by the explosions. On another occasion six drifters were engaged by enemy long-range artillery. For well over an hour shells crashed into the sea, no hit was scored, and in desperation the enemy despatched his dive-bombers. In two formations, 26 machines roared across the Channel at about 10,000 feet. A.A. gunners put up a terrific barrage and two German planes tumbled out of the skies. And as the formations tore off back to France, with British fighters on their tails,

one drifter settled into the water.   Later the same day
mighty detonations heralded the shellfire warning in
Dover: "Shelling in progress: take cover" notices appeared
on the streets as shrapnel showered the town.   In all 184
shells were fired, many of them bursting over or in the sea.

Others of the "little ships" run the gauntlet of German
long-range guns.  On several occasions M.T.Bs., the equiva-
lent of Nazi E-boats, have been bombarded.   Direct hits
with 14-inch shells would shatter such craft.

Dover's tugs, too, the *Lady Duncannon* and the *Lady
Brassey*, famous for their peace-time exploits as salvage
ships, have come in for their share of enemy spleen.

Their crews, comprising a weather-beaten skipper, a
mate, two engineers, three able seamen and four firemen,
know no uniform.   Night and day they stand by: 48 hours
"on," 48 hours "off."   Food, provided by themselves, is
cooked aboard; the "old man" sleeps for'ard in solitary
splendour, but the crew's "'ammicks," bed, and bunks are
tucked into a space far too small to be comfortable.

Sleep is quickly banished when orders for action come
by telephone.   The tug is in motion almost at once.

One of H.M. trawlers has been mined . . . sinking . . .
S O S, S O S by wireless and handlamp.

"How about mines?"

"Can't worry about them," comes the reply.   "Got
to get the cable to her even if there are mines."

This particular trawler was badly holed.   From her
deck nine men jumped on to the tug.   Three volunteers
stayed aboard their wallowing little craft.   Thirty fathoms
of cable joined the two little ships as the tug's 1,600-h.p.
turbines churned up the water.   But the tug was barely
under way when the wheelhand murmured "Think she's
foundering, governor."   Sure enough she was sinking: and
as the tug drew alongside once more and slipped her cable,
three men jumped aboard not a moment too soon.

Good work!

More good work was to follow.   Another trawler . . .
on the sands. . . . Out went the tug.   A nasty sea running.
But 60 fathoms of hawser was passed to the grounded
ship, attached to a towing-hook on the tug.   At this
3½-inch wire link ship's turbines strained.   The tug's stern
rose and fell: the cable, sagging, flopped into the water
with loud smacks, its weight preventing it from whipping

back. Slowly the tug took the strain, then churned forward as the trawler slipped from her bed.

Such work is undertaken within view of German long-range gunners, and Dover tugs draw their fire. When shells come over, the crews kick off their heavy boots . . . just in case! Recently a salvo landed round a tug: the crew fell flat to the deck. Then a message came through to put out to sea: a convoy was being shelled, and a tug might be wanted. . . . A moment later and her temporary berth was occupied by a shell!

The crews have two paramount desires: to bring down an enemy plane; and to feature in a German *communiqué*! "Our coastal batteries shelled a Channel tug to-day."

The enemy has not lost sight of the propaganda value of his Channel guns. They feature in German news bulletins. Photographs purporting to show them in action are released for publication in the Americas and throughout occupied Europe; and once an American Panama "heavy" was represented as pointing across the Dover Straits!

Shortly after enemy long-range guns first shelled the Dover area, broadcasts were made from the gun emplacements. After German artillery had fired heavily on Wednesday, October 30, 1940, German wireless listeners were treated to a broadcast by an ober-lieutenant.

The guns, said the commentator, are on the shore between Calais and Boulogne. Gun sites are in telephonic communication with observation posts: large-scale maps of the Dover area are prominently displayed on their walls. Each "objective" is marked from information provided by reconnaissance planes, distances are clearly and carefully plotted, even to the exact scaling of Dover Harbour. According to the speaker these guns are loaded in the "gun pits," raised electrically, fired, and immediately lowered for reloading. After this discourse came the *piece de résistance*. German listeners were treated to four heavy explosions—"German guns shelling Britain."

The propaganda value of such broadcasts must have been considerable on the Continent at that time. Remember, Britain had never before been shelled by *land* batteries, and Goebbels took full advantage of the position. But the propaganda value of bombarding Britain from a distance of 21 miles must have soon worn thin when German gunners failed to attain material military results.

Meanwhile, the number of south-eastern big guns has increased considerably. *At the beginning of the war they totalled only six.* Then the barrels of "heavies" began to trundle through the streets; and bar and hotel lounge heard of more and more guns and their crews arriving at cliff-tops and railway sidings. The first rounds fired across the Channel answered the initial heavy shelling of the Dover area on the night of August 22, 1940. Since then their thunder has increased considerably.

Roughly speaking, these weapons are divided into two categories: anti-invasion guns, and "counter batteries." Among the latter is the "Bosche Buster," rail-mounted, attended by crews billeted in converted railway carriages; "Winnie-the-Pooh"; and her cousin, "Winnie." There's not a bigger howitzer in the country than the latter—named after the Premier.

It is unwise to probe too deeply into the question of south-eastern coastal defences. Dover guards her secrets well. Especially in its early days as a front line town the Naval and Military authorities did not encourage anyone even remotely connected with Fleet Street. But if journalistic activities are curtailed, Intelligence's all-seeing eyes give one confidence that the south-east's secrets are well protected. On two occasions I have been hauled unceremoniously before Intelligence for a severe "wigging" in a plain-walled room cut from living chalk. Other journalists know that room. On another occasion I was picked up by Dover police, I believe on instructions from the Castle . . . arrested several miles from a spot where two hours previously I had pointed out the position of a long-range gun to a friend!

About this time facts regarding our coastal defences were being released. Journalists were taken over the batteries. We heard "Winnie" had an old boot tied to her muzzle; that her crew, Marines wearing battle-dress, kept 24-hour watches; how "Winnie's" shells, the size of torpedoes, were kept at a constant temperature of 80° F.; how they soared to a height of 9 miles.

Then "Winnie" was brought to the "mike." July 19, 1941, heard her utter a single sentence that rolled and reverberated like thunder: she spoke to a battery of moving cameras and broadcasting microphones.

This was not the first occasion upon which the B.B.C. recorded the roar of Channel gunfire. Some months previously Robin Duff arrived in Dover to record the then frequent Channel shellings. When the bombardment began Duff was flown by plane to pick up the roar of shells. One burst so close to his machine it nearly put his equipment out of action. However, the record was made, the master wax rushed by rail and road to Broadcasting House in time for the 9 p.m. news.

Duff was listening to his record over the wireless when explosions shook the crockery in the restaurant. The enemy was shelling the Dover area again. Duff rushed for the usual cliff-top vantage point known to local newspapermen: by the dim light of his headlamps he read the broadcasting script while 14-inch shells burst on Britain; 4 a.m. saw him rushing his record to the London train, but an air raid developed, and I believe that particular record never reached the B.B.C.

B.B.C. broadcasting of Channel shellings did much to bring the war home to listeners outside blitzed areas: here was the bark of enemy guns recorded from the Front Line where German and British troops were in contact..

However, in some local quarters Channel shelling broadcasts and newspaper write-ups are severely criticised. It is held that they not only encourage the enemy to disprove our frequent statements that "no damage was done," but provide him with valuable information. This can hardly be the case. Press statements to the effect that the Channel is still open to British convoys are not likely to spur German artillerymen to greater efforts; and quite apart from the propaganda value abroad, the news is reassuring to readers outside the Dover area. It is doubtful whether we have ever provided the enemy with information of value to his long-range gunners. Not only does he adopt the services of spotting planes (which we delight in shooting down) and observation balloons (soaring over Calais and sometimes visible from the Dover cliffs), but he can upon occasion see his shells bursting: furthermore, he is almost certain to possess instruments with which to plot the exact positions in which his shells land.

British soldier-scientists keep a close watch on enemy long-range gun emplacements: personnel of the little-known Survey Regiment. With the help of delicate and expensive instruments they locate gun positions, pin-point the arrival of British shells on "the other side." Two methods are employed in spotting enemy positions: sound-ranging and flash-spotting. The former has three objects—to locate enemy gun sites, to range British coastal weapons, and to ascertain what objectives are shelled by each German battery. "Surveymen" work in teams of eight. Within seconds of the firing of enemy guns a recording machine provides a strip of developed film showing the time its microphones received the sound from France. With this evidence the "reader," the "booker" and the "plotter" fix enemy gun positions to within a few yards . . . information they pass to British long-range gunners for future reference.

In the same way the exact points at which British shells explode are plotted with metric accuracy. Flash-spotting is the visual method of "fixing" by the triangle method.

Should cross-Channel invasion (either by the Allies or by Nazidom) materialise, anti-invasion and counter batteries will roar their challenge as never before. But supporting British gunners is what is termed a "freak of Nature": the Channel.

The "Ditch" is one of the most contrary stretches of water. Towards the Dover–Calais bottle-neck Atlantic and North Sea surge. And in the everlasting conflict for supremacy between these two bodies of water is born the Channel's many inconsistencies. Its tides are covered by no rule of thumb. Channel pilots (who, incidentally, were evacuated from Dover's Trinity House after the fall of France) know them for their strength and unreliability. The two main tidal streams, the "up" and the "down" meet off Dungeness. Entering into a struggle for a right of way through the Straits, they push Dungeness's 6,000 acres of shingle towards France at the rate of two yards annually; and in this struggle are born the tide's inconsistencies.

Hitler must have his invasion tide time-tables. They are essential to the successful landing of troops at several points simultaneously. But no Channel tide time-table is reliable. Tides may be an hour early—or late! Northerly winds pile high tides into *high* tides: southerly winds have the opposite effect.

Channel winds can smooth the sea with mellow touch off Calais and whip it into white horses off Dover at the same time. This Cæsar learned on his first attempt at invasion of Britain. Pulling away from France on a silent surface, his legionaries found themselves scattered by the weather on the Dover side of the Straits. The Spaniards, too, learned to respect the Channel winds, which sent part of the Armada to the bottom and chivvied the rest into Calais Harbour.

The currents are things of weird design. They scurry hither and thither, upon occasion becoming lost in or absorbed by larger and stronger currents.

Tides and currents, and to a lesser respect winds, form the sandbanks. Navigable channels through them are constantly changing shape. Those of Prince's Channel, running parallel with the north Kent coast, and those of the Goodwin Sands (opposite Hitler's big guns) are highly treacherous.

The Straits of Dover have other cards capable of topping any held by a would-be invader. Napoleon found that an off-shore wind rendered French and Belgian Channel Ports almost untenable to small craft, while northerly winds, which rise in a twinkling, hemmed them against the shore. It can be seen how the latter wind presents bombers with heaven-sent opportunity to play havoc among craft mobilised and ready for their venture across the Straits.

A calm day, fog, and the right tides provide suitable conditions for a Channel crossing with invasion its purpose. But seldom are these three conditions present at the same time.

Fogs are frequent between September and March. Under their cover an invasion could be attempted. On the other hand Hitler might consider moonlight more suitable to his purposes. The installation of cross-Channel searchlights on the occupied coast tends to confirm this.

The summer of 1941 saw German Channel searchlights used for the first time. . . . "Big Berthas" of about 300,000 candle-power. Their immediate purposes might be interpreted as Nazi nervousness at possible British night raids, or in German efforts to illuminate British convoys negotiating the dangerous Straits after dark. So brilliant are they that one could not hope to manipulate warlike instruments in their glare without the neutralising effect of tinted glasses; and they conjure up a "fantastic picture of a floodlit invasion-arena, with boats weaving and twisting to escape their beams and with bombers raining explosives on an illuminated battlefield."

The guns with which German searchlights operate have other purposes than the closing of the Channel to British shipping. An invasion of the south-east coast would certainly see them used. And just as our mighty coastal batteries could lay "box" barrages on the other side of the Straits (say to clear Calais beaches preparatory to an Allied landing) so enemy long-range artillerymen would endeavour to put their weapons to similar purposes. We know Germany to possess guns with a 100 miles range, and in the event of invasion from occupied France it is conceivable these super-weapons would come into action against inland cities. London would be within their range, though it is generally accepted that their military value to the enemy would be negligible.

December 15, 1941, saw a new gun a-top Calais cliffs pour shells across the Straits for three hours (with two breaks) and the *Evening Standard* stated that it "may have been of heavier calibre than those used previously". Shell explosions sounded louder. If the enemy possesses heavier coastal weapons these will give his "Channel punch" extended range. German coastal batteries supported the *Scharnhorst, Gneisenau*, and *Prinz Eugen* in their dash for freedom, possibly laying barrages in our warships' paths and engaging British coastal batteries which fired on the Nazi battlecraft at extreme range. The noise was considerable; coastal tension noticeable, for, with the roar of planes greater than anything heard since 1940's summer, it was evident an important action was being fought. The day was misty, and in the Dover area the question arose whether invasion was afoot! This hectic action, in which possibly 1,500 planes and scores of ships participated, pictured the conditions likely to prevail if invasion materializes.

## CHAPTER THREE

### EVACUATION: CHILDREN AND ANIMALS

THE Dunkirk evacuation; the appearance of "invasion posters" on walls and hoardings in the south-east during 1940's summer, asking the "surplus" population to pack, set the evacuation ball rolling from Margate to Rye. The threat of invasion was very real. On clear days binoculars brought German tanks, lorries, even troops into view.

They were worrying days. But there was no panic. Folk just packed their bags. Some stored their furniture: more and more empty houses became repositories, those in existance proving inadequate to house the flood of furniture flowing through the streets. Some sought to evacuate their possessions: every conceivable type of vehicle was pressed into service; and removers were booked up to such an extent that during the height of the Battle for Britain I saw an elderly couple seated in a 'bus crammed with furniture, pots and pans, and two "toy dogs." But the majority of people just shut up homes and shops; they considered evacuation a temporary affair. Others preferred to remain in Dover . . . among them my elderly mother.

Leave? Leave her home? And her lovely garden? And her pot flowers? And her "things"? Certainly not! Invasion? Yes, perhaps there would be an invasion. Shelling? Probably we would be shelled. But why should her home be hit from among all the houses in Dover?

Dover was to prove no place for anyone without local ties. The young and the elderly were a liability. It was best they left "the area." And a large proportion did leave.

Homes were shut up at short notice, and countless pets were left to fend for themselves. Scores of cats and dogs roamed the streets during the early days of the evacuation, and a better picture of their sufferings cannot be drawn than that contained in the last Annual Report (dated January 1, 1941) submitted by Inspector Frank Webb to the R.S.P.C.A.

Webb was tireless in his efforts to lessen the sufferings of deserted and wounded animals. He has been seen ministering to them while shell-splinters slapped themselves against walls and road, and while machine and cannon-guns rattled and clattered overhead.

He wrote: "The year has been exceptionally busy. No less than 1,262 animals were dealt with, the large number abandoned by their owners being collected and destroyed. Many animals were rescued from shelled and bombed homes, some were found new homes, the others put to sleep. Of the 148 cats rescued from smashed houses, 18 were found new quarters. 'Minnie,' a cat belonging to a famous ship which was continuously bombed, had a very bad time. When found by me she was in a deplorable state: very thin, with practically all her fur missing, due to burns and scalds; but after treatment and good nursing she recovered.

"During the evacuation of the B.E.F. from Dunkirk, Calais and Boulogne I co-operated with Police-constable May in dealing with 176 dogs that landed with the troops: 146 of these were painlessly destroyed and 30 sent to quarantine kennels. These dogs were of all types and sizes, the majority suffering from shock, some covered with oil from swimming through the sea to the ships, no doubt realising in their own minds that the troops would not desert them. It was very distressing to have to collect these animals from the soldiers, knowing what terrible times men and animals had suffered.

"A large number of animals were killed by enemy action, by shells and bombs; and it may interest you to know that I was the first person to attend animals injured by shells fired from France. The following animals were either killed outright or had to be slaughtered through enemy action: 9 horses, 11 cows, 44 sheep, 16 pigs, 2 dogs, 10 cats, 1 rabbit, 10 chickens; while 3 horses, 15 cows and a parrot received treatment. The area was regularly patrolled."

Many animals accompanied Dover children in the evacuation trains. The first batch of children left us on June 2, 1940. It was a sad Sunday. Men (and dogs) were still arriving from Dunkirk; the town was still sprinkled with French, Dutch and Belgian soldiers and sailors; there were a few civilian refugees—possessing little more than the clothes they wore—who had somehow managed to scramble aboard British ships: one little girl, whose mother had been killed by a marauding German fighter plane, was carried on to the platform on a stretcher, wounded in the arm.

Through this atmosphere, heavy with tension, Dover children marched to the Priory Station. Few parents accompanied them: good-byes had been completed at home, and the children, though obviously bewildered, stood up to the occasion manfully. They were bound for Wales.

My family had long since left me for the tranquillity of a Dorset farm. The period between the Dunkirk Evacuation and the first air raid on Dover saw us ready to leave at an hour's notice. Little Sally, aged five weeks and born to the tune of gunfire, couldn't use her new pram: it was strapped to the back of the Rover. Margaret, aged 3½, raided the back of the Morris for toys. The children's and their mother's clothing was laid out ready to be packed at a moment's notice.

The moment came during a night in May.

Like many other parents, my wife and I had planned against the possibility of air raids forestalling our departure. Sally slept with her; Margaret with me. Each of us planned to rush to the garden shelter with our burdens at the first sign of trouble.

That May night saw enemy mine-laying planes "raid" Dover Harbour. The house rocked as every conceivable type of A.A. gun opened up. Shore batteries and those of the Dover Patrol played an intensely noisy symphony. The skies were livid with colour.

We met in the passage with our burdens.

"They've come!" we said in unison.

"Bombers," murmured a sleepy Margaret.

Unceremoniously the children were shovelled into the shelter as a mighty explosion testified to the accuracy of south-eastern A.A. defences. An enemy machine appeared to suffer a direct hit: it blew up amid a shower of steel "rain."

I returned from the fire station at 3 a.m. to tuck the children into bed while my wife packed a few things. Noon next day saw us heading West. Just West, where little children could sleep in peace—for a holiday, as Margaret thought. She accompanied me in the Rover: Sally and her mother followed in the Morris. Every two hours we stopped to feed a premature, crying baby: for 8 hours she cried. For three hours Margaret slept with her curly head on my knee as I drove. The Rover was not taxed. But the police nodded us on at sight of that tousled, tired head and the heaps of blankets, cots, pots, pans, prams piled into and on to the cars. We saw many others similarly loaded: all headed West.

Next day I returned to a row of childless, womanless houses. The family of five (and twins) a few yards up the road had gone; so had a little lad down the hill. Three men occupied fourteen houses. And we missed the noise and bustle of children and women, perhaps without fully appreciating the loss at first.

Months later a child came to our row.

"Mummy! Come and see these German bombers."

Mrs. Stubbs was plucking vegetables (wearing a tin hat against shell splinters).

"Mummy! Come and see these German bombers. One of them's on fire."

Mrs. Stubbs straightened up. "Did you hear that? A child's voice!"

Dover's bachelors settled down admirably. Many—especially bank men—formed themselves into groups, shared one house: they took it in turn to cook, clean and shop. Men who had never before worn an apron were proficient "housewives" by the time the first shells arrived. Especially was this creditable in view of the fact that the order of the day was dictated by Nazi airmen. It was not uncommon in July and August 1940 to breakfast at ten after all night on A.R.P. duty, to lunch at 4 p.m. after half a dozen alerts (balloon, bombing or machine-gun raids) and to sup any time up to midnight . . . or not at all!

Such conditions were most unsuitable to children. The men who "did for themselves" were denied the pleasure of watching their families grow up, but at least the children were safe. Only once in weeks was it possible to hear piping voices exclaim, "Hullo, Daddy," over the telephone, for during 1940's Summer long-distance telephone calls were as difficult to obtain as radium. Time and again war correspondents hung round telephone booths by the hour in the hope of contacting London; often vainly. It was infinitely infuriating to hear the old remark, "Sorry, there's a two hours delay," when events overhead were screaming to be passed to London. I have waited as much as six hours to 'phone my family in Dorset, only to be cut off at the first exchange of greetings to the tune of "Wailing Willie."

However, even during the height of the Battle for Britain over 1,000 children remained in Dover: not even shelling drove more than a few score of this 1,000 out of Dover. With schools closed, they ran wild. Parents advanced the most absurd reasons for keeping their children by them: "How do we know the sort of home they'd have in Wales?" was the commonest remark. As though such a consideration could outweigh the urgency of evacuating the young from what is the most dangerous town in England!

Quite apart from the lack of school discipline, danger in Dover is ever present. Shells and/or bombs arrived daily and/or nightly during the summer of 1940. Sirens could not be relied upon to warn one of their arrival. At a moment's notice children had to be snatched indoors. And in time the kids became so used to the turmoil of war, with sirens screaming as many as twelve times a day, that they came to accept the conditions as normal. I have seen two four-year-olds playing "bombers" and "big guns" while all hell reigned supreme overhead.

Alderman F. R. Powell, Chairman of the Education Committee, did his best to persuade Dover parents to evacuate their children: Mr. Jones, dynamic Editor of the *Dover Express*, supported him to the full. But the children remained: six hundred infants and 624 children between the ages of eight and fourteen.

The young cannot be allowed to run wild without school discipline and education indefinitely. The Board of Education ordered the re-opening of six schools in October 1941. Six hundred and twenty-four children started to make up for 18 months lost education. In groups of 25 each, two groups at a time, they trooped to schools with shattered windows and broken walls and roofs: at 3 p.m. they trooped out again to play in the streets or the shelters. Many of these kids live in "the caves."

Vivien Batchelor, *Express* staff reporter, wrote from Dover: "I went to look at the caves where most of the children live. I found many pale-faced youngsters wandering aimlessly about. In these caves there are electric light and heating, but even so, the atmosphere was stuffy. In one passage alone I counted seven babies' cots."

Many of these kids had returned from safe areas in Wales. Some parents returned, too: Dover began to fill up again during 1941. And among the voluntary evacuees to return was—my mother. She arrived five minutes before the first Italian air raid on Britain: 4.45 p.m.

Aero-engines throbbed: sirens wailed: a heavy A.A. barrage developed: bombs whistled down.

"My first air raid," said mother, beaming, "what do we do?"

We stopped the car beneath some trees by a military post. Bren guns mounted on nearby lorries pointed towards Italian biplanes.

Shrapnel pattered down and a stick of bombs jettisoned by hard-pressed Italians exploded in the vicinity, cutting the road both behind and in front of the car. A young officer offered mother the shelter of a military "post," but she preferred to watch affairs overhead. The Italians were driven off much more quickly than Nazi pilots would have been in similar circumstances. As is usual in Dover, silence returned as suddenly as uproar broke out. And while the car eased its way past bomb craters mother scrambled into a "bomb hole," bent on finding a memento of the first Italian aerial attack on Britain!

Her reactions to shelling proved similar. They were Dover's reactions.

# CHAPTER FOUR

## CIVILIANS CARRY ON

FOLLOWING the hectic days of Dunkirk the Dover area settled down to a period of uneasy peace. Brilliantly sunny weather did little to dispel mental gloom. The air was heavy with tension. Defeated British and Allied soldiers had swept through the area. German legions, flushed with victory, were but 6½ leagues distant, and the south-east felt like a small boy waiting the cane. "IT" was coming; and feverish military preparations reflected the gravity of the situation. Britain was not ready for the sudden arrival of German troops "across the way." Her army had retreated, but not to "prepared positions." The south-east coast was inadequately fortified; indeed, early in the war the Dover area boasted only six coastal batteries. And frantically she prepared to defend her almost naked shores against invasion.

We saw conditions identical to those preceding the fall of Holland, Belgium and France. Farm carts, decrepit motor vehicles, and hastily felled trees formed road barriers: sandbagged machine-gun posts, flimsy corrugated roofs sagging beneath sods and branches were erected with feverish haste: motor buses spewed swarms of civilians on to the hills to dig tank defences: Bren guns peeped from cottage windows, and armed sentries guarded every approach to strategic points. As many as seven times in eight miles—and especially after dark—motorists braked hard at the challenge: "Halt! Who goes there?" One day a sentry greeted me with the warning: "You'll risk getting a bullet if you don't stop quicker!" Trigger fingers were common in those anxious days, and many motorists were fired on.

Service men and civilians alike were on tenterhooks. The enemy was so close. With binoculars we could see his military vehicles, the vehicles which in one month had swept through three countries. Invasion was in the air, and every alert brought with it the query: "Is this 'It'?" Sirens, whether accompanied by gunfire or not, saw shops, banks, offices, post offices, close their doors. Daily affairs came to abrupt stops half a dozen times in as many hours. With every 'sireen' (local pronunciation) men and women streamed from desks and counters and kitchens to A.R.P. posts. Regular working hours became a thing of the past.

But July 1940 saw the unpleasant period of anticipation pass: enemy planes roared overhead by the score; guns barked and chattered, shrapnel pattered down and machines screamed earthwards aflame. "It" had come: the Battle of Britain burst into swing, the "area" settled down to active service conditions, and civilian life at "Hell's Corner" regained its equilibrium.

We came to expect the first alert following the night's All Clear at about 7 a.m., and periods of comparative peace between 10 and 11 a.m. while enemy machines were licking their sores or reloading across the Channel: that hour saw shoppers scurry into the streets. Subsequent raids usually materialised at hourly intervals, and between them one fitted the day's chores. We settled down to a "raid routine."

People outside "the area" developed a completely inaccurate picture of life in this bomb- and shell-tormented zone. Frequent references in the Press to the hazards braved by the south-east led them to imagine Dover as wrecked, its people white-faced. I remember an old lady who, on my departure from Dorset after a few hours with the family, saying "You poor boy! Back to that *dreadful* town!"

It was not dreadful. True, I left Dover that week-end to the thud of shelling from occupied France and returned as the shellfire warning sounded. But even to-day Dover has not suffered damage to the extent imagined by the rest of Britain; and subsequent to the first shock of bombardment in August 1940 life soon became stable.

Public houses do a roaring trade; evening shellings are their best time: the "Crypt," Dover's underground restaurant, is crammed with khaki, blue and grey uniforms and a smattering of civilians; so is Folkestone's below ground "Esplanade": cinemas and the "Hippodrome" and dance floors are well patronised. Evacuation witnessed many shops close for want of customers, but many of those remaining are glad to sell even during (light) shellings. Such notices as "Our front is down, but our backs are up, so come in and buy," and "Don't mind our blasted windows, we're wide open;" testify to the "business as usual" slogan. Before the Navy- and Press-haunted Grand Hotel suffered a direct hit, George, the head waiter, greeted one with "Good morning, sir. Nice raid, sir! This table, sir, away from the glass."

Early in the shell-blitz bank girls were given the opportunity to leave local branches for less tormented parts. But the Dover area's bank girls elected to stay.

One day a shell found me cashing a cheque. Windows flew into fragments and brick dust invaded the air. Bank records were hurried to safety while cashiers remained at their counters. A girl cashier looked up from handling a bundle of notes to utter one word: "Shelling!" Until it became untenable her home was a basement in the most consistently shelled area of the town. In addition to bank duties she shouldered those of warden, firewatcher, and mobile canteen attendant: week-ends saw her leave an elderly mother—one of the many voluntary evacuees to return home—on her rounds of desolate gun sites and search-light posts with hot tea, buns and cigarettes.

On another occasion a shell fell within feet of her bank. Without warning it dropped from a cloudless sky to send sullen clouds of brick dust soaring heavenwards. From Jack Castleden's cigarette shop I ran across the road to find a man dead by a pile of shattered masonry: hard on my heels came a London war correspondent and a Press photographer. It was reasonable to suppose that this was the beginning of more "fun an' games": German bombardments seldom end with one shell. But the bank's doors remained open and brick dust was swept from counters preparatory to continuing the day's work. After all, perhaps it was the day's first and last shell. It proved otherwise!

My return journey to complete the purchase of twenty cigarettes was interrupted by a second heavy explosion, and into a shop doorway I dived with two soldiers and a woman shopper. Police ran into clouds of brick "smoke" shrouding another bank. A shell penetrated its walls to explode in the strong-room. Miraculously the staff escaped serious hurt.

During repairs much of the bank's business was transacted across the counter of a rival house, but the staff's return to its own premises saw the theory that "two shells never fall on the same spot" disproved. For the second time in a few weeks the bank's routine was rudely shattered by an unexpected explosion. The second shell landed within feet of the first. The latter shattered what windows the street still boasted, scarred brickwork over a wide area, and caused several casualties.

I crossed from the bank to see if my old friend, Mr. Vernon Shone, one of Dover's best-known characters, had escaped hurt. He appeared more concerned with the safety of his antique chairs than with a glass-cut face. "Must get them to the country," he said, helping a young typist sweep glass and plaster from desk and papers. Door and ceiling bore shrapnel marks: window frames lolled drunkenly; and zinc sheets which for about half a century carried the words "ARCHITECT AND SURVEYOR" hung in tatters. •

But two hours later, after lunch, "old Shone," cuts plastered, was back at his desk: so, too, was his typist.

Such is the spirit of civilians under bombardment.

I have seen shoppers remain in the open while shells landed in nearby sectors of the town. A peculiar feature of long-range bombardment is its "local" character. Sometimes we guess accurately which enemy batteries are in action from the particular sectors to receive their spleen. Shells from certain German guns fall in, say, district "A," others in district "B"; consequently shelling does not necessarily disrupt the daily life of the whole community. Were it otherwise the frequence with which the double-alert sounded until recently would have caused a breakdown in daily life.

The enemy appears to have as his main purpose in shelling the town an attack on civilian morale by disrupting everyday life. He plays on the greatest human frailty: fear. But enemy long-range gunners have not attained this object.

The Dover area has not grown contemptuous of shells. Indeed, the knowledge that one's beer may be suddenly spilled and one's sleep and bath and pleasure shattered— the ever-present feeling of insecurity—is disturbing, and Dover admits to a profound dislike of bombardment by

14-inch guns. Discipline provides Servicemen with moral support in emergencies. Not so civilians. They must needs find something within themselves upon which to lean when the first law of nature asserts itself: that "something" has come forward.

One day a high explosive caber sent a small house in the "old" area of the town tumbling down. Rubble littered the narrow street: the stench of explosives hung in the air. Amid this Ypres-like scene A.R.P. workers delved for an old woman known to have been in her front-room shop when her home collapsed. They found her, covered with grime and bruises; and her first remark was a wisecrack: "Any'ow, I got me teeth! Never do for you lads to see me gums!" And a week later this old soul of some 65 winters displayed her "stock" from her daughter-in-law's front window a few yards down the same street. Next her new "premises" a shoemaker plied his trade in the only room left to him.

My diary shows a November Friday in 1940 to have been a heavy day. Conditions had not been very noisy the previous day, and workaday Dover hoped to make up for lost time: but the enemy had other plans. His guns opened up in earnest. Every few minutes four shells landed in a sector of the town suffering severely in previous bombardments. During the height of the "blitz" a shell exploded near the entrance of a cave shelter. It killed an old man walking in the street, caused Dover's first A.F.S. casualty, and battered at the shelter door.

Behind it a score of women and children knitted, chatted, and played: a few jumped up in alarm, but as Fireman Bushell said, "They soon settled down again."

This shelter is situated in a shelling "black area." Certain sectors of the town gained such a bad reputation following early shellings that shops and garages therein were avoided by folk from the "safe" areas. They became black spots. Yet families with homes therein stayed put; and week after week landlords or estate agency collectors knocked on their scarred doors. Business as usual!

I remember "Mr. Mac," one of Kent's best-known and best-loved men—with sweets for the children and gay words for their mothers—saying: "Damn the Germans! Palmerston would never have allowed Britain to be so easily attacked! Damn the Nazis! I'm going to collect my rents."

On more than one occasion a white-haired gentleman wearing peaked cap, canary-coloured waistcoat, breeches, light-coloured spats and a benign smile, knocked on air raid shelter doors while high explosives missiles exploded among British homes. Mr. Mac! Once a shop toppled down within 50 feet of him: Mr. Mac continued business —the poorer by the loss of a friend's daughter. It was Monday: and Monday is rent-collecting day—blitz or no blitz!

We became used to shelling. We accepted it as inevitable. One autumn day in 1940 German gunners lobbed their steel hate into the very centre of Dover. Folk scattered. But not all sought shelter at once. The first salvo drowned noon chimes and for approximately two hours enemy guns roared. Shells exploded in a "lane" through the town, about 400 yards apart. But in the "Crypt" lunch was served as usual to business men, soldiers, sailors and airmen: Mr. Archie Laws, newsagent, stood at the entrance to his shop "wondering where the next one would land"; Mr. Marsh's white head, seen through a minute square of glass in a boarded-up shop front, remained bowed over piles of watches until it became evident the Hun meant business: three Wrens disentangled arms to dive for cover when a shell exploded near the then recently opened "Woolton's Cafe"; and even when the Sugar Loaf's windows fell asunder several women behind them continued to drink coffee: two Corporation workmen continued to shovel road metal into a lorry when a shell landed 300 yards away to injure an old lady.

She died at the Casualty Clearing Station. "Couldn't hope to save her," said Sister Maylan, senior Sister, "with her wounds. Shell splinters make an awful mess of one."

Nora Maylan handled the wounded from Dunkirk; and all shell casualties passed through her small, able hands until she left "the area." There was the Italian fish-and-chip merchant who lost an arm. One day a shell demolished several cottages off the Market Square. I was buying toothpaste at the time, and before the injured man was on his way to the Casualty Clearing Station in Miss Hollis' car the shop assistant was sweeping shattered glass into the gutter.

"No more shelling to-day!"

The Dover Corporation and Council, and the *Dover Express* set the town excellent examples. Dover's Medical Officer of Health and his wife were among the last people to leave the battered sea front for a safer area: the Town Clerk, Mr. Loxton, whose work for the town won him the O.B.E., and his lieutenants are probably busier than they have ever been.

In November 1941 the *Daily Herald* published two photographs of the Mayor of Dover on his re-election for a fifth term, over the caption: "Jimmy the Mayor: The Man Who Serves. Landlord Jimmy Cairns (bluff, hearty Tynesider) of the 'Primrose Tavern', serves you a pint of old-and-mild. Then off he goes to the Town Hall to serve you again—as Mayor of Dover. He puts on his mayoral regalia for the fifth year to preside over a Council Chamber in which he has sat for 20 years. Jimmy Cairns' motto as Mayor of Front Line Town is 'carry on.' He said it again the other day when Dover's 1,500th alert was sounded during a Council meeting. And when the 'Primrose' was badly damaged it wasn't long before Jimmy was back behind the bar, bowler-hatted and imperturbable, carrying on."

Collie Knox drew a living picture of Dover's Mayor with the words: "When I tracked him down I found a burly figure, a man with a downright manner and a 'I've-got-my-foot-in-the-door' look in his eye. 'Can't tell you much,' he said. 'You know it all. We carry on here. The people of Dover are brave, wonderfully brave. Can't say too much for them. Wish people would take their children away. Some of them are bringing them back. But we carry on. Excuse me. Good morning.'"

Lively Council meetings are frequently rendered livelier by enemy action. Alerts no longer see them postponed: raids do not disturb them. One day, during the height of the Battle for Britain, hard-pressed German raiders dropped bombs. Above the roar of aero engines and the crash of A.A. guns their whistle was heard. "I think bombs are dropping," murmured a Councillor. But argument was too heated for anyone to pay him the slightest attention. On another occasion Councillor Eckhoff turned up at the Council Chamber with a face wound sustained in a collision between two fire engines during a night "call." Councillor Eckhoff finds time to attend A.F.S. "outings," collect insurance premiums and attend Council meetings.

The most heated arguments took place over the question of evacuation. Should Dover be evacuated or not? Councillor Walker, blue-eyed and sunburned, "speed-boat merchant" to pre-war holiday makers, summed up the position: "How do I sail my boats in an inland town?" Dover stayed put.

By a cruel twist of fate Councillor Walker was killed sheltering beneath one of his boats when bombs fell on the beach in the first heavy air attack on Dover. The town will long remember that September day in 1940. An Air Force salvage lorry bound for a crashed plane on the Heights gave me a lift into the town. Indescribable confusion. Part of the Grand Hotel lay across the road, a seaman's hostel was "down," the dear old "Granville" (once a popular dance hall and skating rink and military bandstand) was smashed; pubs and shops and houses lay in heaps; a boat flamed on the beach, a Wren-driven naval van overturned, was afire. The wounded, including the girl receptionist at the Grand, were being carried to ambulances. Firemen, A.R.P. personnel and Press reporters surged round the shattered district. It was in this raid that Guy Murchie, American War Correspondent, was wounded; and his dispatch describing the first bombing *and* shelling attack on Dover will long rank as among the most sensational of the war. Murchie showed considerable pluck in contacting London before his wounds were dressed.

Dover stood up to what the *Dover Express* described as a "wanton attack followed by bombardment by the enemy's long-distance guns on the French coast." This was the first occasion upon which enemy bombers and long-range guns tormented Britain at the same time. Barely had the formation of Dorniers wheeled away through heavy gunfire than German shells crashed into the town: their arrival caught A.R.P. services in the open, but not on the hop. Dover had settled down to shelling by then. The *Dover Express* wrote: "Wardens, Rescue Parties, First Aid Parties, Ambulances and Police were quickly on the scene, and everything possible was done to effect rescues, alleviate suffering and convey the victims to the hospital. The first rescue party sent to the scene found civilians, Wardens and members of the Services already doing sterling work. Reinforcements arrived of all Services, and, later, a contingent of a well-known regiment assisted the rescue parties in their attempts to reach those trapped under the huge piles of debris.

"Police-Inspector Grigg was in charge of the incident to co-ordinate the work of the various Services.

"Mr. L. E. L. Jones, of the Borough Engineer's Department, was in charge of the rescue operations, and he speaks very highly of the resource and energy displayed by the parties under his command.

"Conspicuous courage and resource was shown by Stoker Lowe, R.N., who tunnelled under a pile of debris 15 feet high and extricated the licensee, the sole survivor of a well-known inn. The whole time Stoker Lowe was working in an incredibly small cavity in the debris. He was in danger of being crushed by the collapse of a large chimney breast which leaned precariously on the pile of debris which formed the remains of the imprisoned man's home.

"Notwithstanding this heroic act, when it became known that a woman was similarly imprisoned, Stoker Lowe again volunteered to crawl under the debris and locate her. She was finally rescued, after being trapped for $3\frac{1}{2}$ hours. Mrs. Terry, who was rescued, displayed considerable fortitude. . . .

"From the ruins of the same premises Mrs. Terry's $5\frac{1}{2}$-months-old grandchild had been previously extricated without apparent serious injury. The child had been protected by the body of her mother, who had, unfortunately, succumbed to her injuries.

"Many people have been rendered homeless by the raid, and a considerable number of these have lost all they possess. The courage and fortitude with which they have faced their misfortunes are beyond all praise."

Just as the national Press reflects the opinions of the country, so "local papers" mirror the daily affairs of individual communities. Their columns deal with the "little things" that mean so much, the apparently paltry happenings of daily life which in the aggregate amount to a great deal. So it is with the *Dover Express*. I have picked the following items from the latest issue (at the time of writing).

"WANTED. Child's tricycle, chain driven; reasonable.

"TOYS AND CYCLES: Good stocks of toys, few doll's prams.—HILLS.

"WANTED; books and magazines purchased for cash. —Write or call, The Front Line Bookshop, 173 Snargate Street, Dover.

"Seeing is believing.—Luminous leads and collars, the real black-out safety for yourself and dog.—Demonstration at the Pets' Arcadia, 60 High Street, Dover.

"Guns! Guns! Guns! Catapults! Catapults! Catapults! —Georges, Snargate Street, Dover.

"Members of the family, grandchildren of Mr. J. J. Halke, of 34 Salisbury Road, Dover, an old Dover resident, wish to congratulate him on attaining his 90th birthday, wishing him many happy returns of the day, with best wishes for the best of health.

(Salisbury Road has not proved the healthiest of spots since the enemy came to the French Channel Ports).

"LOST. Black and white kitten, answers to the name of 'Pip.'—110 Longfield Road, Dover.

"Ballroom dancing! Mr. Fred Overton, M.I.S.T.D.— arranges private classes for members of H.M. Forces. . . . Club dances organised.

"Every Monday, Town Hall, Dover's most popular weekly practice dances."

*Every* Monday. The enemy is but 21 miles away, but dances will be held *every* Monday! On the average, Dover sees three dances per week, and seldom are they postponed through war causes. One occasion saw the orchestra vie with German gunners as to which could make the most noise: dancers remained swaying to the rhythm of war and a "hot" band!

In the issue of the *Dover Express* before me the Regent Cinema advertises Marlene Dietrich in "The Flame of New Orleans," also "Back Street Boy"; the Granada is showing "Barnacle Bill," featuring Wallace Beery and Marjorie Main; while the Plaza (suddenly as famous for the murder of its manager by a youthful A.R.P. worker as for its position in the Front Line) offers Joan Blondell and Dick Powell in "Model Wife."

As an alternative there is a meeting of the River Women's Institute at "Beresford House."

Such items reflect the "carry on" spirit of a town living under the shadow of German long-range artillery. But turn to the "In Memoriam" column. Here one puts one's finger on the heart of a tormented people.

"In Loving Memory of our dear Dad, W. J. A., who was killed by enemy action on November 13th, 1940.

"In every loving memory of my dear husband, H. M., killed by enemy action November 14th, 1940.

"In loving memory of our dearest Alfred, killed by enemy action November 13th, 1940, aged 16 years."

Mercilessly the Editor of the *Dover Express*, Mr. Bavington Jones, flays parents who risk the lives and the sanity of young children, submit them to bombing and shelling from "across the way." Under the heading, "In the Street," the *Express* says: "They say that parents are to be further encouraged to leave their children in Dover by the provision of Christmas treats."

Particularly is the *Express* concerned with Press reports on the shelling of the "Dover area"; it contends that too many facts of use to the enemy are given away in the national Press. Under the heading "Nota Bene," Mr. Jones writes: "As regards this paper, we make no claim to praise for patriotism when we ourselves tell the enemy as little as possible about what he does to Dover. Living here in range of his shells—which he is fully entitled by every rule of war to fire at us—we have no desire to improve his aim and strongly object to anyone else, except Nazi 'spotters,' doing so."

Whereas few local people were driven underground by the prospect of night raids, shelling prompted many to seek the shelter of Dover's chalk caves or that of garden shelters. German long-range gunners were liable to shatter sleep without notice.

The sudden arrival of a two-gun salvo in close proximity to my home saw me doss down on the ground floor during the late summer and autumn of 1940. Rolf, the child's pet daschound, sidled up to the mattress every time sirens wailed: Pat, the housekeeper's terrier, shared the shelter with his master and mistress. Sometimes the five of us "pegged down" in the Anderson. Then Don arrived. Don, with his bomb-shattered leg. It gave us sleepless nights. Like a steel flail its iron support whipped against one's shins. Stubbs developed a boil on a tender portion of his anatomy, and when steel flail and boil came into contact the moments were hideous! I retreated to my mattress . . . on A.F.S. "off" nights.

Few of those not on A.R.P. duties get up for desultory shelling to-day. They lie abed while high explosive missiles whine overhead to burst inland. After a sharp night bombardment, Mr. V., a prominent local builder, said: "Yes, I thought it time to get up when glass started flying about!"

It did not take other Kentish towns long to claim equal distinction with Dover in the matter of shelling. Gillingham, in mid-Kent, said it had been bombarded; and Canterbury thought it recognised the roar of shells. Certainly shells have landed a little way inland, but not to the extent of mid-Kent.

One evening I listened to a young soldier from an inland village claiming that his game of Bat and Trap had been invaded by a 14-inch shell. But it is more likely that a bomb wrote another paragraph in the 400 years of Bat and Trap history.

Nearly four centuries ago, in the tranquil year 1570, St. Stephen's saw the Beverlie Inn built. In those times the opening of an inn was an event invariably accompanied with much merriment born in free ale, and frequently fostered man's inventiveness. Such, presumably, was the case at the Beverlie. Local legend has it that the opening ceremony was celebrated with the invention of a new game —Bat and Trap.

Unfortunately, I cannot confirm legend, for time has destroyed evidence, as prior to 1824 the Beverlie B & T Club secretaries filched minutes books at the termination of their official office. But there is little doubt that Bat and Trap was popular at least two centuries before the first minutes book was purloined. It has sprung from the very furrows in British soil, and while "the few" fought overhead during 1940's hectic summer, some of "the many" carried forward Bat & Trap's ancient traditions.

Bat & Trap has something in common with cricket, rounders, tip-cat, football and bowls! There's a goal post situated at one end of a "green" 21 yards long by 13ft. 6ins. wide: at opposite ends stand a batsman with a pingpong-like racquet and a bowler with a hard ball weighing 5½ozs. Between goal posts stand the "fielders," their purpose being to prevent the batsman scoring a run for each occasion he swipes the ball between the uprights.

The batsman (usually with beer tankard at hand)

faces a "flap-trap"—a wooden box with a tongue and a movable "trap" at ground level—on to which he places the ball. The latter he shoots into the air by smiting the tongue with his bat (rather in the manner of a small boy playing tip-cat), endeavouring to send it between the goalposts by hitting it as it descends.

It's not as easy as it looks. The batsman must hit the ball by the third attempt or be "out" (rounders-like), while failure to send it between the uprights costs him his "wicket": he can also be caught "out."

It took many years for Bat & Trap to move beyond the mellow walls of its parent inn: shyly it travelled a few miles to the "Falstaff Tap" (built in 1450); but, gaining confidence from its reception abroad, it quickly invaded other inns. To-day, 25 teams (divided into four leagues) compete for challenge cups at the end of a four-months' season in August. But Bat & Trap is still almost unknown outside a country radius of about fifteen miles. It's as "local" as the effects of the shellfire from which it says it has suffered.

Country districts have been heavily shelled. During 1940's harvest the first "large lumps" fired from across the Channel churned up Kentish fields. But farm workers who for two to three months had continued about their duties to the constant crackle of machine guns and chatter of cannon guns, the roar of A.A. batteries and whine and crump of exploding bombs, were not unduly disturbed by shelling —even if their fields were ploughed with shell craters.

An August day saw two farmers reaping while shells exploded among the corn. Britain needed the results of their labour: crashed planes had burnt part of it: incendiary bombs had fired fields here and there. But the remainder of 1940's crop waved, rich and splendid, and, shelling or not, it had to be gathered before rain came.

Many a stirring tale of indifference to Jerry is to be heard in the Dover area's country pubs, where soldiers from lonely "posts," farmers, and journalists with their fingers on the pulse of the people, meet for the traditional old-and-mild. One night at the "Carpenter's Arms"— a minute pub with a well at its entrance and oil lamps illuminating smoky air—old Jim said:

"Aye! Me marrers! Lovely ones they wuz! Oi were just a-going to see them agin when 'woooosh-bang!' And they wuz gorn afore me eyes. An' one of 'em had me little grandson's name cut into 'is skin."

Trouble comes in the Dover area suddenly. One moment one's marrows are intact: the next . . . !

On another occasion—about the same time as a Gainsborough picture was slashed with shell-splinter—a pea-sized piece of shell-shrapnel penetrated a cow's flank. The wound was examined by candle light in a cow-byre at the height of the "trouble." "Couldn't see much," said the farmer. "The beast copped it in the lung and every time it breathed it blew the candle out!"

During the height of the shell blitz, the autumn of 1940, when the Dover area was shelled on as many as twenty-one consecutive days, a shell killed a horse in a field. The farmer moved the remaining three to a "safe" area, and that night a heavy bomb hit their new stable . . . Since the first shells crashed ón Britain in August 1940 nearly 100 sheep have been killed, and many cows and pigs. Inspector Frank Webb, of the R.S.P.C.A., leads a busy and not always safe life in Dover.

August 28, 1940 is entered in my diary as a "heavy day." The Battle for Britain was at its height. Aerial warfare raged overhead: sirens screamed; guns roared: machine- and cannon guns stuttered and stricken planes hurtled earthwards. I spent the whole day at the fire station—it was impossible to get any work done. My diary says: "The day's shooting began at 8.15 with an ME 109's arrival: at 11 others came over, one being shot down, the pilot baling out. At 3.30 I had thĕ pleasure of seeing a German pilot captured on my way by fire engine to his flaming plane."

His ME crashed (aflame) in a field, plunging down almost vertically with a ghastly scream from a height of about 18,000 feet. Military lorries blocked the narrow lane and our "unit" had no option but to await the arrest of the German pilot (badly wounded by his Spitfire antagonist), before it could proceed. And then the Press arrived on the scene with notebook and camera.

The Premier was in Dover that day, August 28, 1940, and he arrived at the scene of the crash by military car before the flames had been controlled. I stood next to him, and his words reflected the general attitude of Dover folk:

"Well, that's *one* German less."

Collie Knox reflected this attitude no less accurately after his visit to the Dover area late in 1941. He wrote in the *Star*: "The sight of (Dover's) beaming postmaster was like a privilege. He revels in shells. One night a shell fell thirty-five yards from the front of his office. Another burst on the pavement. During the war the telephone operators have only gone down to the emergency switchboard seven times. 'Our supervisor,' said the Postmaster, while he was showing me a drawer packed full with bits of deadly metals, 'has just been awarded the British Empire Medal'." Since then the Postmaster has been decorated by the King (February, 1942).

Dover has travelled a long way since the Post Office closed its doors hastily at the sounding of an alert.


# CHAPTER FIVE

## PRAYER AND PLEASURE

CHURCH-GOING in the Front Line town of Dover is liable to sudden interruptions. The last war saw German airmen taking apparent delight in Sabbath bombing. Many a Sunday saw bombs dropped by lone raiders at about the time churches commenced to empty; and if little damage was sustained by church property twenty-odd years ago (though one house of worship was hit twice) the same cannot be said of the present war.

The little church in which I was married suffered from the effects of a 14-inch shell. Old St. James's, one of Dover's finest, oldest churches, has been sorely hurt. St. Barnabas —partly tin-roofed owing to the fact that its builders over-estimated the financial strength of Dover churchmen— is shattered beyond repair. One of Ewell Church's fine stained-glass windows is battered, its flanking walls chipped, its headstones clipped. St. Mary's-in-the-Castle (visible from France with the naked eye on fine days), among the nation's most famous churches, with a chequered career as a house of worship, a stable and a refuse dump, lives beneath the callous stare of German long-range guns.

Yet somehow services continue to be held regularly. People pray and sing, the young are baptised, the loving married, the dead buried—under fire.

The reaction of Dover folk to bombing and shelling is recorded for posterity in one of the war's strangest diaries: that kept by the 32-years old Rev. W. E. Purcell, of Dover's ancient Parish Church. Nearer to the occupied coast than any other British church, its square tower raises its proud head within view of enemy·artillerymen.

In the leather-bound vestry book is recorded the church's exciting history during the noisy months when German aerial legions passed overhead by the hundred night, and day. Entries make strange reading compared with those prior to the spring of 1940. Of these, "EVENSONG —SHELLING DURING SERVICE," is typical. But not often does one come across the entry "Service suspended through shelling." High explosive cabers descending upon the town at a greater speed than sound do not cause the dispersal of congregations unless the bombardment is of the "heavy" variety.

Another typical entry is that for an Easter Day: "Service attended by the Mayor and Corporation—heavy machine-gunning of balloons during service." The enemy very frequently raided Dover's barrage balloons during the summer of 1940. It was not uncommon for half a dozen "balloon pottings" to materialise in as many hours. Through a hail of A.A. fire German "yellow nosed" MEs zoomed, cannon-guns roaring, and if they frequently brought flaming balloons on to our rooftops, we sometimes heard the ghastly scream of stricken enemy planes plunging headlong earthwards. Balloon-potting proved an expensive pastime for the Nazis.

On this particular occasion two Bren gun-carriers parked outside the church opened fire on the raiders as the preacher entered the pulpit. The row was incessant, insistent. But the congregation sang a hymn to drown the turmoil of war. No one left the building: no one turned a hair. And by the time the hymn was finished the noise was over!

Guns blazed, machine- and cannon-guns chattered, flaming balloons left columns of smoke hanging in the air; men died: but within the church folk sang to the Glory of God.

German gunners opened up at us on one occasion ten minutes before a wedding was to have taken place at the Parish Church. The Rev. Purcell, suddenly transformed into

Warden Purcell, went to his A.R.P. post: the bride and the wedding guests retired to an air-raid shelter. But all bad things must come to an end, and half an hour's lull in the bombardment saw the wedding ceremony proceed.

I can quote many instances of Dover folk's reaction to enemy shelling and bombing. Early in the shell-blitz an explosive missile landed within a few yards of the church in which I was married, the church to which we carried our first little bundle of humanity to be christened. Two seamen in the street were killed and the priest wounded in the leg. He appeared less concerned with his wound than he did with the fact that the following day might see him unable to fulfil his duties.

When the Roman Catholic church, St. Paul's, was damaged, parishioners turned out to sweep the floor, board up the windows and repair the roof.

Enemy guns are spaced only ninety yards apart along the French coast between Dunkirk and Calais, but Dover still goes to church.

In the same way Dover's centres of entertainment, though battered, still offer the town first class amusement. The Sea Baths have "gone," the Granville is smashed, but at the time of writing the cinema houses have escaped serious damage. Indeed, since shelling began a cinema gutted by fire before the war has been rebuilt. The "Crypt" still offers excellent meals, dance halls are crammed with Service men and women and civilians, and the old Hippodrome offers twice-nightly shows.

The 'Hip', scheduled for demolition and rebuilding before the war, has probably never been so consistently popular; and certainly it has never known such entertainers as the blitz brought to its small stage.

The *Dover Express* wrote: "Patrons of the Hippodrome will be interested and pleased to know that Mr. Armstrong has received a letter from Vic Oliver, the celebrated stage, screen and radio star, offering to come to Dover for a week in the near future. It is also hoped that Miss Sarah Churchill, the Premier's daughter, will be able to accompany him, so that, following on the visit of Miss Evelyn Laye and Albert Whelan, it will be seen that the management are endeavouring to bring well-known celebrities to this front-line theatre. For the first time in many months the theatre has been able to book first-rate attractions for the ensuing two months."

Early in the war Mr. Armstrong had difficulty in filling the bill every week. Music hall artists did not like the idea of shellfire disturbing their acts. Mr. Geoffrey Warner, comedian-compère, stepped into the breach. Time and again we welcomed him to the dear old 'Hip'. Not content with entertaining 'Hip' audiences, "Warner & Co" invariably gave shows at military and naval posts. Once, his company had just arrived at the hall when a bomb demolished the stage. The wounded received first aid from the show's pianist, Mrs. Geoffrey Warner; the piano was dug out of the bomb crater and carried to a nearby building, and within half an hour the "show was on"!

One of the last privately-owned theatres in the country, the Hippodrome's twice-nightly performances since the blitz began (with very few postponements owing to enemy action) are among the marvels of this front-line town.

One night German long-range gunners interrupted Miss Beryl Reid's (B.B.C. impersonator) performance. She accompanied each "bang" with a titter and the remark "Large Lumps"—local slang for shell splinters! Andrée, a French-Canadian strip-tease artist, did her "stuff" to the delight of the troops and the boom of German guns, and Alex and Marianne danced exotic tangos to the roar of war.

On another occasion Nazi artillerymen opened up just as a comedienne entered upon her first wisecrack. A mighty detonation turned her smile into a sickly grin. She faltered, turned her head in the direction of the explosion, looked at the audience for a long moment and picked up the threads of her story. Subsequently she greeted each explosion with a twitch of her ample nether regions in the direction of "Gairmany," gestures which "brought the house down."

I saw her in the artists' bar during the interval. "Auntie," the barmaid, was serving her a gin. "No," she said, "this is the first time I've heard big guns firing. Yes! I felt like running at first. But no one in the audience moved so I carried on."

The Dover Hippodrome is the only theatre I know where audience and artists can meet during and after the show over drinks. Pre-war the artists' bar was little patronised by Dovorians, but since September 1939 it has proved among the focal points of Dover's night life. Its fœtid atmosphere sees soldiers, sailors and airmen (Britishers, Poles, Norwegians), and sometimes Wrens, A.T.S., V.A.Ds., nurses from the Casualty Clearing Hospital, Fannys, and a smattering of civilians: night after night it's crammed with uniformed humanity, and seldom have I seen it empty even during shelling.

One day I watched high explosive shells bursting round three trawlers. They were hugging the coast between Dover and Folkestone when suddenly the sea round them leapt into the air to the thud of exploding shells. A lorry driver, the passengers from a bus, the driver and conductor, two London newspapermen and half a dozen soldiers from a cliff-top post joined me in front of the "Royal Oak." Silently, inwardly fuming at our inability to *do* anything to help those chaps a mile off-shore, we watched the enemy vent his boundless spleen on those three little ships. Three at a time his shells landed perilously near them. It seemed they must be hit. But once again British minesweepers steamed serenely up-Channel under the snouts of German guns.

-- That night in the Hippodrome's artistes' bar "Tiny," otherwise "Popeye," gave an excellent rendering of himself at the helm under enemy fire. "Popeye" had probably never held the wheel in his life: he was a stoker, but his rendering of a helmsman under bombardment was no less excellent for that fact! Everyone buys "Tiny" drinks. When conversation lags he removes his false teeth, expands his jaw muscles, tucks his lips inwards, grips between them a battered pipe to produce a startling resemblance to Able Seaman "Popeye." I have heard an officer of the "Wavy Navy" (the R.N.V.R.) bid "Tiny" enliven the proceedings. "Stoker So-and-so! Do your stuff." "Yes, sir!" said "Popeye," and out came his teeth! Drinks followed, of course. I have seen "Popeye" piling up the pints while four-gun salvos from Calais guns burst in the town. Such is the spirit of the British Navy.

·. Before, or after, the Hippodrome, Dover goes to (1) the "Crypt," or (2) the Oyster Bar for a meal. Behind the latter's smashed windows lugubrious-looking Mr. Vickery stands to serve. A lobster, three tomatoes and a wedge of lettuce for 3s. 6d. was his charge during the summer of 1941. Mr. Vickery's premises are among the very few to grace a shell- and bomb- devastated street. "Oh no," says its owner, "things are not so bad. This is the nearest oyster bar to Germany, but we keep going."

"The Crypt," too, keeps going. Folk drift downstairs from the "Shakespeare Bars" for a meal, to be greeted by jovial Mr. Jones, its limping manager, who, before bombs terminated the usefulness of the Grand Hotel, managed the latter establishment. Mr. Jones is among the many men to have sought new jobs when enemy spleen upset daily affairs.

In August, 1940, the Grand and the "Crypt" knew hordes of American and British war correspondents reporting on the Battle for Britain. Vincent Sheen, Ben Robertson of the New York *P.M.*, Helen Kirkpatrick of the *Chicago Daily News*, Virginia Cowles of the New York *Herald-Tribune*, Casey, Knickerbokker, Godfrey Winn, and a host of others. Those were furious days for newspapermen. From meals and bed and bath they dashed into the open to watch history in the making as hordes of planes zoomed in battle and guns roared and rattled; to report on the passage of convoys through bomb- and shell-disturbed Straits; to watch and record the sinking of a lightship by Stukas, and to tabulate the quite unbelievable heroism of civilians in the front line. The Grand Hotel is defunct. And Dover's night life has followed Mr. Jones to the "Crypt." At night one meets Reginald Foster of the *Daily Herald* there, probably Ross White, who provides photographs for the *News-Chronicle*, Edwin Tetlow of the *Daily Mail* and Freddie Maher of the *Dover Express*.

Freddie's stick doesn't permit him to play rugger any longer. But it does not prevent him "team secretarying." The war and the blitz saw the defunct Dover Rugby Club revived, and Saturdays witness games between Military, Naval and civilian teams.

During the Battle for Britain many games were interrupted by raiders. I remember Mrs. Stubbs running into my study from the kitchen one afternoon during 1940's autumn. The opening stages of the Huns' aerial assault on Britain saw dog-fights taking place so low that the flame from cannon-guns was plainly visible. But as British A.A. guns got the measure of the enemy and British fighter formations grew in strength, so aerial battles took place at greater heights, until by the autumn the contestants were invisible except when the sun glinted on their wings. But still lone raiders managed to skim low over the roof-tops to rake Britain with 'lead.' Mrs. Stubbs was highly excited. "Quick! Quick! Come an' see! They are gunning the footballers." We dashed into the garden, which adjoins a sports field, to see players flat on their faces while Bren gunners stationed on the 'touch-line' engaged the raiders. For a few moments guns spluttered. The enemy was driven off. The tin-hatted referee blew his whistle and the game continued!

On another occasion a mixed hockey match between Wrens and Naval men was interrupted by Messerschmitts; and on yet another occasion bombs dropped on a Service pitch during a football match caused several casualties.

But the Britisher *will* have his sport. Brook House tennis courts are still popular: shells and bombs have fallen within yards of bowling greens, but bowls' clubs are still well patronised; darts' clubs are popular; association football and rugby and hockey in the winter, and cricket in summer are played regularly. And if enemy bombers and long-range guns disturb play the temporary return of peace sees games taken up where they were left off.

## CHAPTER SIX

### MOTORING UNDER SHELLFIRE

SOUTH-EAST Kent, with its rolling hills and white cliffs, with its lovely orchards, hopfields, its ancient castles and churches linked to Britain's earliest days of Christianity, with its good roads and popular beaches, was a favourite haunt of pre-war motorists. They visited us in their hundreds. When war broke out they came to the south-east less for its scenic beauties than from a desire to "see the war." The Contraband Control Station, with its scores of merchantmen sheltering behind "the banks" off Deal, proved a great week-end attraction. And there was always the possibility that ships of the ever active Dover Patrol would stage a show. South-eastern cafés and hotel-restaurants did a roaring trade.

But with the advent of German hordes "across the way" conditions altered radically. Motorists were no

longer welcomed to the south-east: without a yellow pass
gummed to windscreen you could not cross an invisible
line drawn parallel with the coast some miles inland.
Purely "pleasure" vehicles were driven from the roads.
Not a vehicle (bar Service and essential services vehicles)
is abroad without a permit, and permits are not easily
come by: cars for which permits are not granted lose
essential parts against police receipts before they (the
removed parts) are sent out of the district for the
duration.

Road barriers and armed sentries add their quota to
the motorists' burden: many drivers were fired on for
failing to answer challenges early in the war; and many a
Messerschmitt roared over country roads, guns blazing.

Dover was taking no chances in those early days of
threatened invasion. The Police and the Military and Naval
authorities were acutely "fifth column conscious": all
roads were guarded and watched.

Once I was picked up by the Dover Police—I believe
on instructions from the Castle—an episode which had its
lighter side; for where is the junior who would not delight
in causing his chief's arrest?

Mr. H., my boss, came from mid-Kent. New to Dover's
war-time ways he accepted with alacrity my suggestion
that we inspect a coastal "Boche Buster." We stopped the
car *en route* to a beauty spot patronised by film stars and
business magnates in pre-war days. There was no one in
sight. I pointed out the gun and we drove off.

Two hours later, emerging from the underground
"Crypt," we felt the arm of the Law.

"This your car? Then will you come with me to the
Police Station?"

Our action earlier that day had been noted: the regis-
tration number of the car reported to the authorities.
And if I suffered no discomfort through "arrest," Military
posts between Dover and a mid-Kent town 55 miles
distant were warned to stop Mr. H. He reached home
rather late!

Early in the Battle for Britain petrol became scarce.
The answer, "Sorry! No petrol to-day," was as common
as 1942's version regarding cigarettes. And during alerts
it was impossible to have one's tank filled: sirens saw all
petrol pumps run officially dry.

But by the time the Battle for Britain was a fortnight old south-eastern motorists had settled down. I have seen tin-hatted taximen, bus drivers and Wrens driving calmly along while overhead all hell raged: gradually, as Dover became used to the "new order," civilians did not even forsake the top deck of buses when "shrapnel" pattered down. One noon I saw a young woman lean forward a fraction of a second before a jagged piece of A.A. gun splinter whipped through the flimsy roof to bury itself in the upholstery.

Only when enemy long-range guns took up the Hymn of Hate did buses cease to run. The arrival of "Shelling in progress: take cover" notices sees bus services suspended, and one has the option of dining in the town or walking home. Most folk walk home, dodging under cover when necessary.

Inevitably motorists have close shaves. Jerry is very near. A friend of mine was driving quietly along when a shell burst almost in front of his car, hurling it across the road, riddling it with splinters. His companion lost a foot, but miraculously the driver escaped with minor injuries. During another bombardment an acquaintance, bound for a town flanking Dover, received a shell splinter in the arm. High explosive cabers were ploughing up the fields on both sides of the road, and he had the option of returning home or continuing on his journey. He chose the latter alternative.

Those of us reporting on the war from the Dover area (even free-lances like myself) drive flat out for the "Royal Oak," midway between Dover and Folkestone on the cliff road, when the enemy vents his spleen on the south-east. Abbots Cliff offers a grandstand view of the French Channel coast, and from its crest have been recorded for posterity some of the most exciting episodes of the war. One day in July 1940 I was "bussing" past the "Royal Oak" when suddenly the bus swerved to the kerb. Machine-guns crackled as we tumbled into the road. Two planes, separated by a bare hundred yards, zoomed by at roof height. The first: a Messerschmitt; the second, a Spitfire. Stabbing flames leapt from the latter's leading edge as the pilot sent a final hail of bullets into his smoking adversary. Both machines dived low over the cliff edge; only the Spitfire rose again into the air. We scrambled on to the cliff top in time to witness Folkestone fishermen pick up the German pilot.

One night, after the shelling of a British Channel convoy I repaired 'to the "Royal Oak," leaving the car parked outside, its sidelights facing across the Straits. A moment later an irate Home Guard entered to greet me with the words: "Don't yer know them lights can be seen from Germany? Want a —— shell over?" I felt he was a little too careful but then Dover is acutely shell conscious, and British cars *can* be seen from the occupied coast.

Dover garages have suffered severely in the shell-blitz. Several have been hit, and there have been casualties among the ranks of mechanics.

One garage, situated in a shelling "black area," has suffered a direct hit and two near misses. Time and again its Manager, Mr. J. D., has threatened: "One more shell and I quit." But the second shell saw him rent as a temporary "works" a barn in a frequently-shelled country district; and the third shell prompted him to convert an underground petrol tank into an office, stores-room and workshop. Enemy bombardment sees the staff scuttle underground. Miss C., J. D.'s diminutive secretary, types at her desk while youthful mechanics, bent almost double owing to the low roof, continue at work. With the All Clear "J. D. & Co." emerge, and work proceeds in glass-less, battered, roofless premises (not so long ago), littered with shell-shattered cars, until the next double-alert.

A.R.P. services have the rough end of the wedge as regards motoring under shellfire. Time and again demolition squads, fire-engines, ambulances, have been called upon to drive through areas under heavy fire, and many have been the acts of bravery. Men and women continue at the wheel.

# CHAPTER SEVEN

## CIVILIANS IN UNIFORM

"ME. 109 due east. Me. 109 due east. Over." A young Spitfire pilot reports to his squadron leader. Through the loud-speaker we hear the answer.

"All yours. All yours. Over."

"Going into action.  Going into action."

The flip of ping-pong balls ceases: we crowd round the wireless set, awaiting news of yet another aerial battle. Soon, perhaps, we hear good tidings.

"Me. 109 destroyed.  Me. 109 destroyed.  Over."

"Nice work!  Nice work!  Congrats!  Congrats!  Any damage?  Any damage?  Over."

"No damage.  No damage.  Returning base to reload. Returning base to reload."

During the Battle for Britain south-east Kent heard many such conversations between fighter pilots prowling the heavens.  During alert periods the wireless set at Dover's A.F.S. rest room was kept tuned-in to the wave length shared by "the few."  Once we heard a Hurricane pilot, "lost" at 30,000 feet over the Channel, requesting help.  On another occasion two Empire pilots had the following conversation:

No. 1.  "Where are you?  Where are you?  Over."

No. 2.  "Over the Folkestone Odeon.  Over the Folkestone Odeon.  Over."

No. 1.  "Join you there for grub to-night.  Join you there for grub to-night.  Seven o'clock.  Seven o'clock. Over."

No. 2.  "O.K.  O.K."

Overhead, gnat-sized specks zoom and roar, resembling jewels as the wings reflect the sunlight.

"Going into action!  Going into action!"

Cannon and machine-guns exchange compliments. Briton and Teuton speak in a common tongue.  And we press round the wireless set while A.A. guns engage yet another enemy formation; and Polly, the A.F.S. pet, flaps his wings and imitates machine-gun fire.

"M.E. destroyed.  M.E. destroyed."

Soon the Control Room's "in" phone tinkles.  Miss Flack repeats the message as she jots it down.  "Enemy plane crashed at 'X' Crossroads.  Corn on fire."

Eight men—some in uniform, some in "civvies"— clamber aboard a fire engine, fire bells clang: 18-years-old Driver Stoker lets in the clutch: we roar into the street, arrive at the scene of the crash before cannon-gun shells have finished exploding.

The Dover area's Civil Defence Services have weathered the storm admirably.  They boast three George Medals and

several B.E.M.s at the time of writing. Gone are the days
when those who joined A.R.P. services risked the accusa-
tion of endeavouring to evade military service; the time
has passed when Civil Defence uniforms struck the less
patriotic as rather funny, and the antics of their wearers
as funnier still.

We faced many difficulties in the early days: lack of
equipment, lack of trainers, lack of volunteers. But
enthusiasm was not missing among those who joined up.
On the shoulders of men and women who for months gave
two nights a week to instructors rested the responsibility
of training the scores of volunteers clamouring for the
right to help when Czechoslovakia's fall unseated General
Apathy; and those demanding pink forms to sign in
September 1939.

We learned the game from each other. I came to like
and respect the men—miners, bank clerks, shopkeepers, a
Town Councillor, bus drivers, dock hands, seamen, a
publican, roadsweepers and public school men—who week
after week turned up after hard days' work to climb ladders,
roll hoses, crank engines, tie knots, clean and scrub and
polish, and to attend lectures. Gradually we learned to call
the "spout" a "branch," we learned to "run one into two"
and "two into one," and to carry injured people in pre-
scribed fire brigade fashion: we adopted firemen's jargon
at every opportunity; and if anyone wanted advice Old
Man Vigor was glad to help.

Vigor was 70-odd. He recalled nights when his wife
harnessed the horses while he and his crew dressed: his legs
bore the marks of flames: he had "fire" in his blood. He
was the most regular attender at what he called his "re-
fresher classes." No one liked to tell Old Man Vigor he
was too old to play at firemen. But the time had to come.
Mrs. Vigor met her husband at the fire station after his last
"class." He left us. But Vigor was not to be denied a place
in Britain's A.R.P. services, and months later an old man
wearing a warden's armlet signalled our engines to hydrants.
It was Fireman Vigor!

At the other end of the A.R.P. age scale are the Clarke
twins—sons of a baker-warden. A.R.P. messengers, aged
14, they were presented to the Premier on his first visit to
Dover as the country's youngest blitz veterans: up to that
time the Clarke twins had not missed "duty" once.

September 1939 saw the south-east "waiting for it."
When sirens wailed we rushed on duty—certain that at
last "It" had come: night after night we stayed up till
dawn, straddling upturned boxes, fire pumps warmed for
instant action, telephone switchboards manned.  And the
days following night alerts found us in no condition to
work well.  Later, Dover evolved a system of "off" and
"on" nights: on "off" nights we stayed abed while the
other fellows manned the fort.

But "It" did not materialise for months.  Our first
reflection of war was the Dunkirk evacuation: our first
contact with it when A.R.P. and A.R.S. personnel played
a small part at Dover's Casualty Clearing Station—
disposing of amputated limbs and dressings, and helping
to move the wounded.

The wounded flowed from big and small ships along
piers to hospital beds.  A constant stream of mutilated men
passed through the tireless hands of Sister Nora Maylan.
And those of us who helped will never forget either the
energy of nurse and doctor or the fortitude shown by the
wounded.

Two Auxiliary Firemen were detailed to lift a wounded
Guardsman.

"Mac slipped his arms under his shoulders.  I took his
legs," said my senior officer.  "But when I lifted my arms only
the bedclothes came up.  The poor devil had lost both legs.
'Under me behind, fireman,' he said, 'me legs is evacuated.'"

Another soldier, his right leg missing, said he'd "have
to play left back next season."

This was our first taste of war.  More was to follow.
German bombers came over: scores of them.  The Battle
for Britain gained momentum, and as A.A. guns roared
and planes screamed down in flames, so fire engines, demolition lorries and ambulances raced through the streets.

Previous to the opening phases of the Battle for Britain
the A.F.S.'s sole experience in firemanship had been "wet
drills," and on one occasion a fire started for its special
benefit in an area scheduled for demolition. I remember
how a fireman detailed to "rescue" Algy, the fire brigade
dummy, from a flaming attic, reported to the officer in
charge with the stuffed effigy of Hitler slung over his
shoulder: "Here he is.  His brains are leaking out."  Poor
Algy's head had come into contact with a nail and its saw-

dust stuffing left a trail across the road! Those were great A.F.S. and A.R.P. days. But this was the real thing. The heavens were full of fire and thunder.

Those early days in the Battle for Britain found many of us despondent. Dover knew few war correspondents until July 1940. Reginald Foster was among the first to arrive and practically the only news to be telephoned to London was the destruction of British aircraft. Time and again fire brigade "units" raced to flaming planes bearing the R.A.F. insignia.

"When do we have to put a Jerry out?" was on every fireman's lips.

The explanation was probably that stricken enemy machines headed for occupied aerodromes—some to crash in the Channel—while our own boys turned for English fields. Later, when massed raids developed, we had our Jerries—any number of them.

But the real test of the A.R.P. services came when first enemy shells landed from occupied France—August 1940.

The south-east had planned to meet heavy aerial attack; its A.R.P. Services and A.F.S. were well trained and keen: but the men and women who formed their personnel had not anticipated shelling by long-range guns. The first salvo to explode in Dover caught them unawares, and they did not take kindly to the "new order." But that inner something made itself apparent; and soon bombardment was accepted as a necessary adjunct to Dover at war.

On a September evening in 1940 the enemy opened up at Dover. Shells ripped into the town. The fire station shuddered to the roar of 1,500-lb. explosive missiles: on the station floor men awaited the call to go out; upstairs, telephonists sat by the switchboard.

"All men over the road to shelter. Two messengers stand by the switchboard." Firemen obeyed the Chief. He went upstairs. "All telephonists over the road. Patrol Officers Spicer and Dane take over phones."

Momentary hesitation among the girls prompted the Chief (one of the first G.M.s of the war) to repeat his order. Then Miss Flack, daughter of our ex-Chief, stood up: "We'd prefer to stay here, Sergeant Harmer. This is our job." But Harmer was already in front of the switchboard —"over the road at once," he retorted.

Dover firemen soon became shell-blitz veterans: so did

A.R.P. personnel. They were all "at the ready and damned keen to get going" when Dover suffered its heaviest day's shelling (to that time). Bombardment commenced at the height of morning shopping, and for 2½ hours German gunners sent up to four-gun salvos across the Straits every few minutes. The roar of bursting shells and the crack of A.A. guns engaging a Nazi spotting plane mingled in an unholy symphony. About this time—1940's autumn—the enemy made use of artillery spotters, but so many were shot down that he adopted other means of learning where his shells landed—among them artillery balloons on the occupied coast.

On this occasion a "black area" received a high proportion of shells fired. A dozen fell within a radius of 100 yards. Roads were torn up or blocked, or littered with rubble: telephone wires drooped from smashed supports: the stench of explosives mingled with columns of brick dust.

Early in the shell-blitz wardens frequently mistook these funereal columns for smoke, and fire engines were needlessly sent into black areas.

I remember Fireman F. being detailed to confirm a warden's telephone message that the Burlington Hotel—the tall building which first struck the eye of pre-war tourists returning from Calais—was afire. Fireman F. was a motor-cycle messenger. It was he who did such sterling work during the first shelling of Dover.

"Yes, sir," said Messenger F. We went outside. He straddled his motor-cycle; but he did not move off.

"What's the matter?" I asked,

"Can't do it, sir. My nerves have gone. Can't go down there."

I don't want to preach, but it appears to me that so long as man exists solely for himself, a part of his being is smothered and the vent through which that something bigger than his everyday self can emerge is corked. Peace forbids the majority opportunities of drawing the stopper. But war frees the vent, and through it flashes that picture of man which subconsciously he most desires: for some a fleeting picture of sudden heroism, for others a grand tableau reflecting supreme patriotism, chivalry and duty towards fellows in torment. Months of shelling and bombing saw that something bigger than anything we had previously known, or even suspected, emerge in shining splendour.

Time and again men too young or too old to be in the Forces, women, and even youngsters, grasped that golden opportunity by the horns to win, if not self-praise, then something far greater . . . the praise of their fellows.

Not one shelling saw bravery at a premium. Fireman F. had already demonstrated his qualities as a civilian on active service. He could not help being shell-shocked.

Tommy Johnson, grinning, musical-minded Tommy with a taximan's cap because "his 'tin' didn't fit," took Messenger F.'s place. He went into the black area.

About that time a special constable ran into the open towards a wounded civilian. The latter was standing in the open, "wondering if the fun was over." Four to a salvo, roughly ten seconds separated the arrival of each shell of each salvo. The first of a salvo crashed into "X" Street: its three brothers were due within 30 seconds. From the shelter of a doorway the "Special" saw a man sag to the ground.

His subsequent actions prompted my senior officer, Section-Officer P. Bainton, to enquire his identity for decoration.

"A tall, fair chap of about 30," he said. "Bravest man I ever saw. Ran from cover into the open at the exact spot where the next shell was due to land in a few seconds to rescue an injured bloke. Even when the rest of the salvo came down he didn't turn a hair. Deserves the G.M."

"X" Street was in the black area. Its surface was littered with debris. Down it Patrol-Officer Spicer, in peace time a milk roundsman, took his unit. Shells exploded nearby as his men dismounted: they sought shelter from flying bricks and shell splinters before entering a nearby building. Whilst there, a shell penetrated its walls.

Spicer returned to Main Station: "Small fire reported by Leading-Hand Larkin: electrical."

"How did you put it out, Larkin?" asked Sergeant Brown—the new Chief, and, like his predecessor, the holder of the G.M.

"Well, like this. I sees a fire, a little 'un. And I sees a pudding on the stove. So I empties the pudding water on the fire and puts the saucepan back on the stove, neat like."

One of the shells which interrupted Larkin's unorthodox method of fire-fighting killed a man. Two civilians died that day.

Later, British batteries replied to the German fire: and

that night the rumble of British bombs drifted across the Straits from the direction of Nazi gun emplacements.

To-day those guns are constantly bombed. British squadrons pay to them almost as much attention as they did to German barge concentrations during the summer and autumn of 1940.

Dover's A.R.P. services adapted themselves to the "new order" remarkably quickly. They became used to shelling, and even heavy bombardments do not interrupt billiards, ping-pong and musical practices. Fireman Tommy Johnson (banjo), and Fireman Forth (violin) accompany L/H MacDermot and Fireman Bushell's voices. They're among the A.F.S.'s concert party personnel. Time and again Mac and his pals entertain at military and naval posts, and when last I saw the "Tommy Johnson Quartet" it was practising for a B.B.C broadcast. And it practised to the tune of shellfire.

Bombardments are the A.F.S.'s swear-box's best moments. Given half-a-dozen good "shows" before Christmas, and there's enough to provide a station beano for the men! Until it was stopped by Authority, "Tich," in peacetime a baker, used to scoot round the corner to his father's shop for a tray of cakes during long shellings. More than once Tich's buns have had hazardous journeys to the fire station!

"Off duty" men meet at a pub near the fire station, together with "rescue men," wardens, and first aid workers . . . "just in case Jerry gets really rough."

Women play a prominent part in Dover's A.R.P. services. One night shells were landing thick and fast when Miss A. came up to me with a cup of tea. All hell was abroad.

"Where's the stuff landing?" I queried.

"In 'M' Road," she replied. "Dad has left, I'm glad to say. But I hope the tortoise is all right. He's in the garden, you know."

Yes, Dover carries on.

www.ingramcontent.com/pod-product-compliance
Lightning Source LLC
LaVergne TN
LVHW051802080426
835511LV00018B/3387